DON'T WISH YOU WOULD HAVE

Choosing Resilience in the Face of Loss

Carri McQuerrey-Funk

For wholesale inquiries, please reach out to carri.funk17@gmail.com

Published by Radiant Publishing
Paperback ISBN: 978-1-963922-16-5
Hardback ISBN: 978-1-963922-17-2
Ebook ISBN: 978-1-963922-18-9

First Edition
Printed in the United States

DEDICATION

For my beautiful daughter Madison, my cherished nephew Noah, and my beloved brother Eddie—your absence is felt in every breath, but your love remains woven into my soul.

This book is for you, and for all who have walked the impossible path of grief. May these words serve as a light in the darkest moments, a reminder that love does not end—it transforms, it carries us forward, and it binds us forever.

You are missed beyond measure. You are loved beyond words.

To my parents, Ed and Vicki—your unwavering love and strength have carried me through the darkest nights. You taught me resilience, compassion, and the meaning of unconditional support. In my grief, I have leaned on the foundation you built, and for that, I am forever grateful.

To my children Tyler (his wife Elaynna), Alex, and Ellie, and my grandchildren, Ava and Aria—you are my light, my purpose, and my reason to keep moving forward. In the depths of sorrow, your love has been my anchor. You remind me that even in loss, there is still laughter, joy, and the promise of tomorrow.

To Maddie's dad, Wally—through the unimaginable loss, through the pain that words cannot hold, you have shown strength beyond measure. Your presence in this grief has been a testament to resilience, to the depth of a parent's heart, and to the enduring spirit of the love you have for her.

To my closest friends, Brian, Erica, Kelly and Kim—my unwavering anchors in the storm.

Through the depths of grief, you have stood beside me, held space for my sorrow, and reminded me that even in the darkest moments, love and laughter still find a way. Your patience, your kindness, and your quiet strength have carried me in ways I can never fully express. For the late-night talks, the gentle encouragement, the moments of silence when no words were needed, and the endless reminders that I am not alone.

Thank you for walking this journey with me. Your friendship is a gift beyond measure

To my fiancé, Ed—my safe haven, my steady ground, my unwavering heart. You have held space for my grief, honored my pain, and reminded me that love does not end—it evolves, it strengthens, it carries us forward.

Your patience, your kindness, and your quiet strength have been a gift beyond measure. You have walked this journey beside me, not to fix, not to fade, but simply to stand with me in the storm. Thank you for the love that endures, for the promise of tomorrow, and for the beautiful life we continue to build together.

ENDORSEMENTS

Don't Wish You Would Have is a deeply moving testament to the power of resilience and faith in the face of unimaginable loss. I've known Carri McQuerrey-Funk through our professional relationship— she was the customer, and I was the service provider—and I've always appreciated her warmth, kindness, and approachable nature.

Through others, I came to learn that Carri had experienced the devastating loss of her daughter. Having recently lost my own brother, I decided to reach out rather than avoid the subject. Carri graciously shared Madison's story with me and sent information on furniture safety and tip-overprevention—resources that reflect the very heart of her mission.

That conversation marked a shift in our relationship. Shared grief created a deeper understanding, and I saw firsthand the strength and purpose that Carri carries with her. I'm grateful she has written this book, which so openly reveals the depth of her character, shaped by tragedy yet driven by purpose.

The loss of her daughter forever changed how Carri sees the world— through a lens sharpened by sorrow but focused on healing, service, and hope. Her faith anchors her. Her resilience lifts her. And her words offer a lifeline to anyone navigating grief. Carri's perspective is not only unique—it's painfully gained and profoundly powerful.

This book is a gift to those walking through loss, and a reminder to us all of what truly matters: our faith, our family, our friends, and the power we hold—even in our darkest moments—to choose how we respond.

Endorsement by Joe Laughlin
Chief Executive Officer, TSI

I have known Carri for over 15 years. From the moment I met her, it was friendship at first sight. I found myself drawn in by her warmth and keen ability to capture your sense of curiosity about Carri…knowing it goes deep.

In time, you come to realize the tragedies and triumphs that make up Carri.

This book exemplifies Carri's life story, through her darkness and how she found the light, the truth, the wisdom….to share it all. Its very essence is sharing and 'Carring'.

The concept of 'Don't Wish You Would Have' has 'Carri's' meaning beyond words.

Endorsement by Brenda Meli
Chief Executive Officer, SAM Inc.

I've heard Carri's story many times while working alongside her. She practices what she speaks in this book and you can see how it helps. I remember the first time I heard her story while in the workplace and my reaction. It was amazing how she doesn't make it uncomfortable and let you see the good that came from Maddie's life. I've watched her do this over and over with other people. Carri is a tremendous leader through her ability to help others and commitment to improvement which is demonstrated by her willingness to open up here. I'm so happy she is sharing her experience this way.

While I don't believe I've ever experienced trauma like many others, I'm so grateful I've read this book. I feel prepared for when something happens and know I can come back to it when needed. I recommend this book to everyone, whether you've experienced loss yet or not! Best wishes to all of you,

Endorsement by Brian St. Louis
Colleague and Friend

We all talk of responding to life's ups and downs. The clichés are abundant…"pick yourself up off the canvas" and "get back on your horse" and many others. But what about true tragedy, those unexpected, haunting moments we never allow ourselves to imagine? When those moments happen, there are no catchy sayings or poetic words that make a difference. The sense of loss, guilt and isolation can overwhelm even the strongest among us.

But thankfully there are a rare few, like Carri McQuerrey-Funk, who find a way through that darkness to make the world a brighter place. Carri's story doesn't represent a silver-lining, but a guiding light for those who are dealing with the unimaginable. Starting with a parent's worst kind of personal trauma and through incredible transparency, accountability and vulnerability, Carri offers herself as an example of how to live life again. She has turned her pain into purpose in a way that truly helps those who need it most. Her journey is emotional, poignant and inspiring and I truly appreciate her willingness to share it.

Endorsement by Adam Cohen
Chairman & CEO, PCA Global Ventures

To be able to take a horrific event in your life, one that is so very destructive and profoundly life- changing, and grow through it, transforming and learning and thriving and finding meaning in the disaster is one of life's biggest feats. These are gifts that can come... if we open our minds to it. The resilience of the human soul is astounding.

Meeting Carri after the loss of her daughter, Madison, and after the loss of my son, Brandon, was one of many healing moments in my grief journey. I see it as divine intervention and true inspiration from one grieving parent to another, a priceless gift. I am grateful to have this connection, and readers of her book will no doubt be touched and transformed by Carri's perspective and her raw grief that has brought her and so many others to a place of deep insight into what the human spirit is capable of. What she brings is a true gift in a world that so desperately needs it.

Endorsement by Candi Tolson
Founder, Brandon Tolson Foundation (BTF)

Funk reminds us that no matter what experiences we endure in life, we always have a choice in how we respond to them. By doing that, death shifts from being an enemy to being one of our greatest teachers.

Endorsement by Janet McGee
Licensed mortician and co-founder of Parents Against Tip-Overs

Carri's story is gut-wrenching and courageous, but what sets this book apart is her refusal to sugarcoat grief or tie it up in tidy lessons. She writes with raw honesty, humor in unlikely places, and a stubborn drive to find meaning. If you've experienced loss—or love—there's something here for you. This is more than a memoir; it's a lifeline.

Endorsement by Stephanie Eidelman
Founder & CEO, Women in Consumer Finance

There is a reason we call her 'Candidly Carri'. Carri meets you where you are and brings you through the journey of her deep and personal grief and loss. She does it with heart and love and also perspective, grace and power. The powerful words on the page bring you into the moments alongside her, and she keeps it very real every step of the way. And, in true Carri style the book isn't just about the events in her life but how they transformed into the perspective she created from them, as she walks through the other side of them.

'Don't wish you would have' is a message of a woman who experiences profound losses and has a deep desire to make a change not just with herself but with others around her, and people she hasn't even met yet. What a blessing to see deep inside these experiences and have the steps laid out for anyone who goes through grief to support them to get to the other side of it.

Thank you Carri, for sharing Maddie's message through your words, she is alive in so many people.

Jessica Burrell
CEO Next Level Trainings

Table of Contents

INTRODUCTION

There are a few things in life that are guaranteed. The unexpected is definitely one of those. Some may encounter seasons of loss, health issues, and surprises that are not always good. That's just part of life. Even the most well-equipped and well-to-do individuals can't prevent the unexpected; it's just humanity. Maybe you picked this book up because of something unexpected in your life. Right now, you're shaken to your core and don't know what to do. Believe me, many can relate. Unfortunately, it's the subscription that we all signed up for, paying taxes and living a life of momentary affliction in one way or another.

If someone were to gauge the experiences of our peers and put them all on a grading scale, we would all testify to similar situations that we can relate to. We're not all that different. Some, of course, are more risk-averse than others, but for the most part, we behave similarly. So, if we were to experience similar afflictions, traumas, pains, and disappointments in life, then what makes us different? Why do some people respond to unexpected life-altering situations the way they do? What makes them tick so they can come out of the throngs of existence with a head on their shoulders and a heart that's filled up, ready to tackle the next day? These are some of the questions I asked myself when I was in an unexpected place in life—a place I could have never imagined being in my wildest nightmares. I experienced something that changed everything I knew about myself and my world, and it's the process that I went through and what I learned that I want to share with you.

See, we all have a choice in how we respond to life. The choice is the difference-maker, and it is what either makes someone isolated and independent in their plot, or someone who decides to move out of their experience into another. One thing this makes me think of is specific mothers who have used their tragedy for good. Think "back up cameras," think "cordless mini blinds," think MADD (Mothers Against Drunk Driving) … It's evident that someone could make it through trauma and have a healthy and helpful mindset on the other side of life. Life is never made unbearable by circumstances, but only by lack of meaning and purpose. Were these moms just made different? Or are they just like us? Did they make different choices with their mind and heart, and therefore, profound resiliency was displayed for all of us to see? I believe so.

If life is bound to happen to us, then why don't we respond in a way that makes us a better person because of it? I'm bound to uncover this in my life, and I'm determined to pursue it for myself, my family, and those around me. What other real choice do we have but to face our fears and stare into the abyss of the unknown with what we've learned so that we can change our future? It sure beats wallowing in our pity, watching Netflix all day, utilizing bad coping strategies, and feeling like we're going nowhere in life.

There's an opportunity available for each one of us that's unique to us. No one else will get this opportunity; that's how special it is. It's when we encounter a moment that shakes us to our core, that breaks us in half, that we could have never expected—and we have a choice at that fork in the road to decide how we want to change our identity. Do we walk down the path of being a perpetual victim, or do we decide to become someone better for it? Does it somehow find a way to become a catalyst for who we could become, or has it cemented our future and ruined everything? The opportunity to use our stories for something great is upon us, and it's time for us to go through the process of healing, perspective, and growth to choose the right path. It's time for us to turn our pain into something meaningful. I feel that you'll realize the untapped potential that you have inside of you as we go through this process together. Don't worry, I'll be your guide.

THE CALL

I got the phone call that no parent wants to receive when they're at work. "There has been an accident, and you must leave now." Thoughts and emotions swirl a million miles a minute when you have something like the word 'accident' or 'emergency' in your mind. It's hard to even comprehend various scenarios about an emergency unless you've already considered them before. Most people draw a blank and are filled with anxiety. I could not comprehend what I was about to experience, and I endeavor to share my story with you so you can get something out of it. First, let me fill you in on the backstory so you understand what brought us to this fateful day.

A perfect world with the proverbial white picket fence

Was my life perfect? No, but I liked to think of my life as complex and ordinary. Conventionally unconventional. It had its ups and downs, but I had a great childhood—an amazing father and mother who loved me. My dad is a retired officer in the military, and my mother is a retired NICU nurse. We were able to travel around the world when I was young, living in Japan and then finally landed in Virginia. I married young and had my first child at 23. Unfortunately, Brian and I divorced when our son was three. As relationships go, sometimes they just don't work out. I was grateful to be able to remain friends, and still are friends, with Brian and his new wife today. Divorcing so young was tough, but I owned my part and decided to love again. I remarried at 28, and in 2003 had my second child. My new husband was a bit older than me and we knew if we were going to have kids, we needed to act now. Alex was the perfect addition to our family, an amazing little brother for Tyler. Fun fact though, I would always say we will have babies until we have a girl, which was a tall order! Well, after Alex, I had a miscarriage, but then I got pregnant with a girl, Madison, and she was born in September of 2005. Our perfect little dream family came true!

She was everything you would want in a little girl—she was awesome. She grew up with two big brothers. She loved Elmo. She loved wearing dresses. She loved what she called "Yip" (lip) gloss. She always had these cute little piggy tails. She was a doll. Of course, she was everyone's favorite. Madison was the light of our lives. Loved by all who knew her.

Co-parenting and nannies

Of course, having three kids now, my house was busy. I always maintained a healthy dynamic with my ex-husband since I had a child with him, and so I stayed in close contact with his family. You have to be connected and closely aligned when you have a co-parenting role. We raised our kids amicably—as I said, conventionally unconventional. My new husband was an active father and a phenomenal stepfather to Tyler. My ex-husband was very much involved in Tyler's life as well. We worked super hard on the proper dynamics so the kids would not even realize that the cordial partnership and involvement of all of us parents was abnormal to societal standards. We worked very hard to make sure the kids only felt love and support from all of us. That is the main point

I'm trying to make, ex or current, all parents were present and active for all of the kids.

We had a busy work schedule, so I was always wanting the childcare to be done in my home. We went through a few iterations of what that might look like and landed on a live-in nanny. She was a young lady in our church and we were excited to have her. We needed someone we could depend on because we both worked high pressure jobs outside of the home, which included a lot of travel and a lot of hours. This was a short-lived experience.

Over time, I'd come home from work and start noticing things. Odd little things, things we couldn't overlook. We started putting it together and realized it wasn't a coincidence; she was stealing from us. We had to let her go. We had no other option because the breach in integrity was too much. We couldn't risk what else could be hidden in the gap with her. How safe are our children? It makes you wonder what else they're doing wrong; the trust was broken.

This left a gaping hole in our childcare needs. Because of my amicable relationship with my ex-husband, I invited my ex-sister-in-law to help us. I figured she was related to my oldest son, and I had a good relationship with her. She was highly regimented, organized, and extremely loving. That temperament is very appealing when you have a chaotic and busy household. She watched over the kids and kept detailed records in a notebook of everything that took place, including the activities they did that day, what they ate, etc... I never felt like I missed a thing. It was comforting. I always knew what they had for breakfast, what they had for lunch, what kind of bowel movements they had, and if they learned anything that day. She always tracked diaper changes, bottles, etc. We didn't have to guess if they were regular or constipated when we got home. If you ask me, it's a nice little cherry on top when you're a parent. This was such a relief. Looking back, it was this attention to detail and rigor that would provide a source of comfort when having no idea at this point what lay ahead.

This part of the story is one that I've been scared to share for a long time. The guilt and shame have overcome me many many times. Please let this be a lesson, one I didn't learn early enough. When we came home from work on October 22, 2007, our nanny shared a picture of Madison she took earlier that day, covered in diaper cream all over her face. We all got a laugh out of that because kids do unexpected things. It was also a little scary because that's potentially toxic. Where did she get it, and how did she get it? We knew she was being watched when she wiped diaper cream all over her face. We always kept the diaper cream on top of her dresser. Our nanny expressed her concern that Maddie had been able to get to things on the top of her dresser, she was worried about the safety in that. So Maddie's dad and I went into the bedroom and looked at the dresser, trying to solve the mystery of how she got the diaper cream. Madison was two, an explorer at the time. We shook the dresser and tried to figure out how she could climb it. Open the drawers, it makes a ladder. It's pretty heavy though. No way this thing is moving. It was a tall chest of drawers, five drawers. We both agreed there was no way that dresser was tipping, so that was settled and we went on with our night. Little did we know that we were less than 24 hours away from the darkest days of our lives.

October 23, 2007

Typically, I'd wake up and rush off to work, but on this particular day, I felt like making breakfast for the kids. When I make breakfast, I make cheesy eggs with bacon grease, not eggs with butter like our nanny would. The kids preferred my cooking. I think that's natural, nothing better than mama's cooking. I'm not exactly sure why I went out of my way to make them breakfast that day, but I was glad that I did. I'm glad I stopped and took the time. It was my last time making Madison's breakfast.

I was in the middle of a typical workday when I got a surprise call from my dad. He said, "You know I'd be rich if I got a nickel every time I thought of you." I thanked him and let him know that's a nice thing to say. So sweet to get a call like that because it was unexpected. It really made my day. This is important, and I'll come back to this later in the story, but the timing of his call to me was no coincidence. Later that afternoon, around 3 p.m. or so, we got an emergency message from our executive assistant. The nanny had called; there was an emergency with Madison and we needed to get home right away. (When the dust had settled many months later, we realized that the actual time that my dad had called me coincided with Madison's time of death.)

I'm totally confused. I'm like, what the hell? We lived three miles from the office, so we got in his truck and raced home. All the while, I'm hoping maybe it's just a little burn, a broken leg, or something we can manage. I'm praying she's okay. I was praying to God that all things would be okay. We all make it through emergencies all the time with kids. Hopefully, this is just another thing that we can figure out.

It's hard to describe the emotions that I felt while driving at the speed of light to get back home. Everything slows down. I could see my thoughts flying by, like the closing sequence of Star Wars. It's like a dead space in the sky where you can feel your heartbeat, and you're aware of your breathing pattern, in and out, in and out. The void of what could have happened was so great that time stood still. I couldn't hold two thoughts together during that rapid car ride that took a lifetime.

We pulled into our neighborhood and turned onto our street, and we immediately knew it was much worse than we had anticipated. There's no way she just broke her leg. The whole street was lined with fire trucks, police cars, and ambulances. It looks like a scene from CSI. Shock started setting in my body, and I was filled with adrenaline. I felt chills from my head all the way down to my toes. It felt like the weight of the world was on top of me. I was about to vomit. As we were pulling in closer to our house, an ambulance started to pull out and leave. I jumped out of the truck, and I ran as fast as I could, screaming at the ambulance.

"Stop! Stop! Stop! I think that's my daughter in there." My gestures and screams got the driver's attention, and he stopped the ambulance.

He comes to the back of the ambulance and tells me, "Ma'am, we have to go."

I said, I think you have my daughter in there, and I want to see her.

He replied with, "No, ma'am. We have to go."

I was frustrated, "Why can't I go with you? That's my daughter in there."

He said, "Ma'am, you cannot go with me. We have to go right now; we have to take her," and so they left with the lights and sirens blazing.

I was broken. I think I knew right then that she was dead, but I was still holding on to hope that they were rushing to save her.

Frozen in time

No words can actually describe what a parent feels in these moments, but I'll try. The flood of emotions started to set in. I was standing there watching this ambulance drive off with my child, and I am so confused. I'm broken. I'm crying profusely.

I finally took a few steps towards the house after being frozen in time. They walked me inside my house; my four-year-old was still there, with the nanny and a police officer. I hugged my youngest, my son Alex, and I asked what was happening. The nanny said the dresser had fallen, and when she went to get Madison up from her nap, she was under the dresser, and her face was blue. She said that her color returned as soon as she got the dresser off her. So she thought there was hope. She started doing CPR and called 911. Madison threw up during CPR, which, at the time, we thought to be a good sign. All the while our four-year-old son is witness to all of this. He is 21 years old today and tells me he remembers this vividly, and remembers being sent upstairs away from the commotion when paramedics arrived.

The police officer asked me if she could ask me a few questions. I nodded yes.

"What was your daughter's name?"

"What do you mean? What WAS her name? Her name IS Madison. Is my daughter dead? No one has told me anything."

"No, no, I'm not saying that; I'm not saying that. I just want to know what her name is."

I repeated myself and said, "Her name IS Madison."

Then the officer asked when her birthday was. At that moment, I held on to an ounce of hope because the officer hadn't said that she was dead. Then the officer said, "Let's go to the hospital."

We initially started walking back to the truck, but the police officer told us to ride with them in the back of their police car. Either they're being nice to help us out, or we're under investigation, and when those doors shut in the back of the police car and you can't open them from the inside, you know you're under investigation. I've never been more scared in my life, I couldn't think about it for too long. I just wanted to reach out to everyone I knew. I reached out to those friends who I knew were close to God. Closer than I was. People whose prayers God would listen to more than he'd listen to mine. I called my dad. I knew my mom was out of town, so my dad called her. I called my friends and told them which hospital we were heading to.

We pulled up to the hospital, and the feeling going in was strange. It was like everyone there knew that we were Madison's parents, like they all just had a conversation about us. They were spaced out every 20 feet or so, and they would look over and gesture or whisper to each other as we walked in. It was like they had played a game of telephone about us, letting those in charge know that we had arrived. The officers and staff kind of shuffle us in a room. We sat there for two minutes, waiting in silence, surrounded by our work friends and my dad. Then, the ER doctor came in. She knelt in front of me and with a sense of urgency said, "Are you Madison's parents?" We said yes. She said, "Your daughter is dead. Your daughter has died. We did everything we could to save her, but she didn't make it; we're getting ready right now so you can go see her." She was so matter-of-fact, so blunt, and then she was gone.

I had triggering thoughts immediately. The first thought in my mind was all my failures—every time I let myself down and let my family down. Broken commitments, broken promises. I thought back on the moment when I was broken, stupid, and reckless, and I was bargaining with God. When I was out pursuing selfish ambitions and desires and sinning against myself and God, I said to myself, "What's the worst thing that could happen? I may lose myself, or I may lose someone else in my family for my actions." The worst thing that could ever happen to me is if one day when I have a child, something happens. I'm talking about 20 years prior, I'm talking way before I ever had kids, and the memories came rushing back. I know, stupid thoughts right… How could I remember them, but I did. I immediately felt punishment for the sins of my past. I was reaping what I had sown many, many years ago. I'd forgotten about that moment for a really long time. My subconscious was flooding my mind. It reminded me of every good and evil thought flashing before my eyes. I guess it was my mind's best attempt to solve my dilemma. I was paying a steep price. Maddie's dad was paying a price, which he didn't do anything to deserve. I've spent the last 18 years struggling with this truth.

What has happened to you?

The things that have happened to us, like losing a child, health issues, car accidents, and even marital separations, can all destroy us. Perhaps you've gone through something similar—a loss or setback that's unspeakable, one that you can't possibly fathom. If you haven't, you're one of the lucky ones; perhaps you've made some really good decisions and kept your inner circle small. But for the rest of us who have experienced a form of significant loss or pain, we're often forced into this season by our circumstances. We don't get to choose when we want to have these low moments in life. Where our heart is ripped out of our chest, and we're laying there on the floor wondering if anyone's going to help us. It just happens. Life just happens. At the moment, it seems there's no plan for how to respond to these things. In some factual sense, that's true. However, those who have been through trauma and made it out on the other side tend to have a few things to share to get us back to a place where we're able to function, where we're able to live again, where we're able to love again, and maybe even a place where we can thrive again.

I know there are some of you reading this right now who have been through significantly worse situations. You have your version of Maddie's Message that you could probably share. Maybe your events are unfolding before your eyes, and you've reached out to this book for help. Good for you. There's tremendous insight in the following chapters that will help you. I wish I had something like this for myself when the ER doctor looked into my eyes and told me that my daughter was dead. Little did I know that I'd be going on a journey in my life to sort through this pain and trauma and try to make sense of it.

Even if your trauma is 25 years old, if you haven't processed your pain, then you could be experiencing the same trauma just as if it happened yesterday. Maybe you're like me: you bottle up the pain and hope it goes away. Well, after 18 years, it doesn't just go away. You have to deal with it and process it in a healthy way. There's a process to go through that will help you heal properly and create a plan to build resolve in your life. I understand the emotions. I've had many strong emotions enter my mind and my body during this time. Those emotions speak very loudly, and they demand that they be heard. Understandably so. There's been significant trauma, and those emotions are correct in their message. Amid those intense emotions, though, we need to be able to reach out our hand and ask for help. The way we do that today is to open up our minds a little bit to the help that we might need because we might be surprised about what's actually helpful. If you're reading this right now, then you're doing exactly what you should be doing: trying to understand ways to heal, rebound, reimagine your life, and take the next step forward.

The first thought you may have, as I did, is can anyone relate to my pain? The answer is yes. Seeing as how this planet has somehow housed over 8 billion others over the course of time, many people can probably relate to our situation. You're not alone. Regardless of what you've experienced, getting help is possible. We may not be able to fully rectify every situation, like I can't bring back my daughter, but the decisions I make from this moment on can somehow make me a better person and help those around me. At some point somewhere, whether it's in the middle of the grieving process or afterward, I'll be given a choice. Do I wish to stay here forever as a victim of life circumstances, or do I want to learn something from this and turn my pain into purpose? That is what I asked myself subconsciously, and it's my question to you. I know you might not be able to answer that question now, and that's totally fine. But I want you to know what's possible before we begin the grieving process.

GRIEVING PROCESS

Our minds are tricky. We can start the grieving process before confirming any of the details. The conversations and scenarios that we play in our minds are quite untethered and elusive. When I got that phone call, and I left work, I had already started grieving. I went into the traditional stages: denial, anger, bargaining, and depression. These stages can be repeated many times.

You can go through all of them in five minutes or five seconds. But how do we know if we've appropriately grieved to position ourselves for better outcomes after the fact? I guess the answer lies in how often we return to the stages of grieving. See, most people get into a cyclical loop when grieving. They don't progress into acceptance from a place of health, and so they're guaranteed to return to the cycle and start all over again. It's not an easy process; as a matter of fact, no one probably wants to go through grieving, but we're required to if we're alive, and how we progress through grieving determines the person we will become on the other side.

As of today, I have processed the story about a thousand times in my mind, or maybe 10,000 times. I have it on replay, so I can watch it every now and then to see if the results will change. It's like watching Groundhog's Day with Bill Murray; anytime it replays again in my mind, I see how I might have responded differently in this scenario.

Unfortunately, the real outcome never changes, but that doesn't stop me from trying. Although ruminating may seem natural, it must be done in a healthy manner that actually progresses us forward. I've definitely done things incorrectly for a long time, and I hope to share those events with you so you can get something out of it. The goal of this chapter is to make it through the grieving process.

As I jump back into Maddie's story and highlight elements of my journey, I want you to glean from my life and apply whatever transferable goods there may be to your own story. You know your trauma, you know your loss, and it's my hope and intention that you're able to be honest with yourself about where you're at and put forth a plan of action that will get you to take the next step forward. Everyone deserves to make it through the stages of grieving and become a better person. But it's going to take a lot of work to get there. If you don't know trauma or loss yet, then this will be invaluable to you because it'll save you years of going around in circles, tormenting yourself with "what ifs" and "shoulda, coulda, and wouldas."

You don't always get to choose when grieving starts

Regardless of whether you want to start a grieving process or not, when trauma hits, it has already started. When most people think of grieving, they think of crying and letting go, something that you would probably see at a funeral. The grieving process is much more robust than that. It's not just about letting go. It's about rebuilding yourself, rebounding, reflecting, reinforcing, reimagining, and bringing resolve to your new life. I believe that the grieving process is actually tied to our identity, our emotional well-being, the decisions that we make after trauma, and how we choose to live our lives thereafter. Proper grieving should make the most use of your pain and turn it into good in some way. We must embrace the loss we've just encountered before taking the next step or taking our next breath.

The hospital staff came in and mentioned to us that they were preparing her daughter so we could see her. Shortly after, they asked us to follow them. So we walked into the big emergency room, where curtains were the only walls between my baby and others. I walked up to her, and she looked perfect. She was beautiful. She looked just like my baby, just sleeping there, as always. She didn't have any bruising. She didn't look hurt, and she definitely didn't look dead. She looked perfect. Honestly, I didn't know what to do at the time. I've never been in a situation like this before. Thankfully, some friends and family, my dad, and our local pastor showed up. I remember clearly making sure that everyone got their time with her. They came out of their way to see us, so I wanted to ensure they saw her. I asked everyone who came if they wanted to hold her one last time. And people took turns holding her. It felt like the right thing to do.

By the time it was my turn to hold her, she was cold. She was like holding a stiff board. She was heavy, and this was the most terrible experience. I remember crying and rocking back and forth. I would look at her face, examine her body, and kiss her. I knew this moment was significant, so I studied my daughter; I tried to memorize everything about her so her image would be burned into my mind and I would never forget it. I hated being there in that moment, yet I couldn't seem to put her down.

I started to apologize to her. I told her I wish this never happened. I told her how much I loved her, over and over again. Then my mind started reeling again, what I did and didn't do to protect her. WHat I could have and should have done differently. My mind would go from affection to guilt, back to apologies, back to guilt, back to affection. The cycle was endless.

The pastor interjected and said something very profound to me. He pulled me aside while others had their time with Madison. He said, "Carri, I'm going to tell you something, and this is not an easy thing to hear, especially at this moment. You will need your OWN people to lean on, and it can't be your husband. He's not going to be able to support you through this. He's going through it himself as well. He is grieving. He will let you down if you have unrealistic expectations of him at this moment." The pastor also pulled Wally aside and told him the same thing about me.. This was helpful to me because of the tremendous burden that I felt at that moment. I don't know how much I could give to anyone, including my kids and my husband. Knowing that I would need help and that others were recognizing that, was helpful.

Who knows how much time went by before the detectives came in and wanted to speak with me and Wally. So I said my goodbyes, and I went into an interrogation room. They began asking me questions about Maddie, her babysitter, our life, and our home, what I knew and what I didn't know. They made sure to split us up so that they got our stories separately and then could cross-examine us. Talk about adding trauma on top of trauma. I had nothing to hide, of course. I shared everything with them, but it was terrible, being questioned while the detectives tried to determine if I was responsible for my daughter's death.

After they concluded their rounds of questioning, the hospital sent us home. By the time I made it home, it wasn't more than 10 minutes later when I received a phone call from the donor procurement company (Life Net Health); they wanted to harvest organs and tissue from my daughter to be used by kids in need. I said you can have whatever you want. It won't bring her back, so take whatever you want. This experience was odd. The questions you have to answer as part of the vetting process was weird for a two-year-old child. That was the most icky part. They asked me a bunch of ridiculous questions. Let's just say it was not easy answering these questions because she's a baby. Nevertheless, I answered the questions. It was about four months later when we received the news that Madison's heart valves had been placed with two separate children, one in Texas and one in Alabama. We were officially a part of the Donor Family. Being a Donor Mom is one of my proudest titles.

What's next?

I remember standing in my living room, asking myself what to do now. How do you go on with life when you come back from the hospital after something like that? You can't drop everything. I still have kids. I have a spouse. I have a job. Everybody still needs me. I have to figure out how to just keep everything moving forward, and maybe one day, I'll take some time and figure out myself and sort through my pain. One day, but that day will have to wait.

I still have to plan a funeral. Before Maddie died, my life was already maxed out with work and family, but now I feel like my workload has just doubled in an instant. When will I get a chance to actually grieve the loss of my child?

Looking back now, I realize that grieving is not just about letting go and moving on but about every moment and every little decision that we make after trauma or loss takes place. Here are the traditional five predictable paths of grieving.

- Denial
- Anger
- Bargaining
- Depression
- Acceptance

It's extremely common to have a relationship cycle with these stages—both within yourself and with each person in your life, especially those closest to you.. The goal in our understanding is for us to see that there's more of a predictable process that most people go through. It needs to be considered as a stage or a moment in time. This doesn't mean that some people will go through denial the exact same amount of time and frequency as they go through anger. Rather, we should consider them normal responses and behaviors to something significant.I went through many stages of grief.

Denial

I definitely started off with denial, as most do. At this stage, we feel like we're losing our foundation. We can't believe that what's happening is happening, and it's so much easier to just be in denial because reality is overwhelming. If the emotions are too strong and the thoughts are too negative, it's helpful to be in denial for a little bit. Denial saves us in some ways. When we identify questions about our situation and ourselves, we start to move forward in our healing journey. The internal sign of our progress is that we're not remaining in our denial forever, and we should graduate from this stage and not return to it.

We should always be mindful that our progression through the stages will differ from others. People who hear the news for the first time will likely start at the beginning of their grieving journey, and it's important not to return to the beginning when you've seen progress. Allow them to have their own grief process.

Anger

Anger is definitely more of a common response to unexpected loss and trauma. Anger is also a required stage in our healing. The demonstration of anger means that you can recognize the loss you feel and the responsibility for your life and those around you. Anger at yourself is often disguised as pain. The way we exhibit our pain is by getting angry. It's like we're venting in a particular behavior. It's common for people to get angry with themselves and the people around them to express feeling unsettled and insecure about the future.

Rather than burying and ignoring the anger, we should redirect it to a more beneficial outcome. It should move us to change rather than divide us from ourselves and others. My most common approach to anger was to deal with myself. My mind can be harsh at times and beat me up. Many people choose to get angry at God because of the unknown. Ultimately, they're just expressing pain that hurts and don't know what to do. We should allow anger to help us reach the next step in our journey rather than destroy our future.

Every good thing is worthy of being protected and fought over. This is why anger is a necessary requirement in relationships. It means that you have something to fight for, you have something to love. Because of this, you're going to utilize this emotion in a positive way. Don't be scared by emotions. They are just trying to communicate to you.

It's hard to have linear, productive thoughts when the emotions are overwhelming and loud. Oftentimes, in a heightened state of emotion, the logical side of our brain shuts down. Many refer to this as the fight, flight, or freeze scenario. Needless to say, productivity is probably at its lowest when our emotions are at their highest. Have you ever tried to have a conversation with someone who's screaming at you? That's not very helpful or productive. The same applies to someone who experiences loss and pain. They can't think clearly for many reasons, including that the frontal cortex is shut down. For us to logically walk through grief, we need to quiet our minds and emotions to sort them out and answer their outstanding needs.

Bargaining

Bargaining, in its traditional sense, is exchanging one thing for another. We do this psychologically, trying to negotiate with the intangible situation. If I were to act like this, then the outcome would change. If I behave differently, then the outcome will change. These are two examples of bargaining. I remember being in the car on the way over to my house when I got the news and also when I was in the hospital, and I did everything I could to bargain with God to see if I could fix the situation. This is where all the what-if statements come from. If only we could change the outcome, I would behave differently. It's natural to negotiate with the pain we feel, which is part of the process. The positive sign of being in this place rather than being in denial is that you're aware of the situation and are not ignoring it.

Bargaining is a normal sign, but it's not a healthy foundation to build on. We don't want to stay here because if we remain in this place, we are removing ourselves from the ability to have responsibility moving forward.

Depression

Depression gets a bad rap because of its effects on us, but if there is one positive indication of depression, it means that we're back to our current reality. We're not trying to negotiate with invisible walls that can't be moved, nor trying to pretend or deny our reality. This is the stage that weighs heavily on us. The dark clouds come in, and we can't think clearly. Sometimes, we have such strong emotions that we don't know what to do with them. We decide to shut down all of our emotions, and we become numb. Rather than trying to solve the reason why we're here, we often medicate ourselves in a perpetual state of hormone and chemical inhibitors. Sometimes medication can help these things and bring us to a better place. Sometimes, medication makes it worse. The thing we should always know is that depression after loss or trauma is normal and appropriate. If you were to go through the loss that I went through, and you didn't experience depression, then there might be something wrong with you. The goal, again, is to not stay here. We need to not sit in our state and make it permanent. We need to find a way through it, which often requires lots of help, therapy, counseling, and life coaching. I never went to counseling myself, neither did Wally, but we did make sure the boys were in peer groups with other bereaved children. These seemed to be helpful at the time, but we did not make a consistent effort for this to continue as they got older. Something I wish I had done differently for them both.

Acceptance

The last stage of grief is acceptance. Please don't confuse accepting a loss with approval. It doesn't make what took place all right or permissible. Accepting is simply coming to terms with reality, the reality that there was a significant loss or trauma, and you're aware of it. Your emotions have processed the pain, and you're physically mindful of how you should move forward. Nothing about acceptance makes what happened okay. We can still be angry at what caused our situation, and the anger would be justified and considered a form of wisdom.

Acceptance is learning to live with your new reality. It takes a lot of adjusting, and every day might not be sunshine and butterflies. It's a permanent change, and it won't always feel good. However, the more we're willing to embrace our current reality, the better off we will be moving forward. Finally, acceptance allows us to embrace our past and live in our present fully. If we refuse to accept our past, we will perpetually live there, and our current state will suffer.

No one will notice my pain

I ask myself, when will I actually get a chance to grieve the loss of my child? If I'm honest with myself, I don't want to grieve for my child. I just want to bury all the thoughts and emotions and hope and pray they don't come back up. I want to bury every thought and feeling I don't like as deep as it will possibly go so that no one will see the pain that I have inside. I intend to do that because it's what I've always done. We all have reasons to hide behind our insecurities and fears for better or worse. For me, burying my emotions was not a new concept; as a matter of fact, it was an art. I had perfected it. We convince ourselves and our minds that if we ignore a thought or an emotion, it will just go away. Of course, that's a lie. It just manifests in every other area of our lives.

We become short-tempered and a little snappy at those we love and care for, which erodes our relationships. Looking back now, I'm not surprised that my marriage did not make it through the loss of my child. The trauma was too great, and I imagine my contributions to the relationship weren't the best either because I was in need of help myself. I take full responsibility for this.

When you bury your emotions on the inside, you stay a little depressed all the time. Maintaining an equilibrium of being numb or becoming aloof is not uncommon. Your actions mirror your not wanting to be seen, so your personality becomes fickle. You may carry this disdain and resentment and alienate yourself from others. Or, like me, you pretend—you fake being happy. There is nothing like putting a little makeup on and getting into something flashy to wear, to try to make people think you're okay. It's easy to convince ourselves that they don't know what's going on inside. No one will notice my pain, is what we tell ourselves, and for me it was mostly true. Very few people understood the pain hiding beneath the surface.

Everyone will notice your pain. They just may not choose to participate in it. They may ignore you or follow the lead on your needs, whether it's to keep yourself busy or for them to entertain you, but to think that they're not recognizing that you're in pain is a fallacy. There's no hiding the fact that we've been through serious trauma. It's like we're holding up a sign or walking around with the word drawn on our forehead. People might not exactly know what's going on, but they can see that something's wrong or different. Your behavior might be off; you might be shortsighted in your ability to plan with them and act strange and standoffish. It's better to confront your pain so that it doesn't modify your behavior forever.

I'm too busy to stop and heal

The cyclical side of grieving incorrectly is like that Journey song: *'The wheels in the sky keep on turning...'* We get caught if we don't heal correctly. A never-ending cycle of spinning in circles. The grieving process should be a forward motion from where we are today to where we're going. It's been 17, almost 18 years, and I sometimes feel like I am still healing. I know I am. I'd be the first to say I went through unnecessary pain and conflict because I refused to address grieving and its proper stages when I should have. I did my best to care for those around me but often neglected to take care of myself. I just kept myself busy, but the trauma that I thought was buried deep always found a way to creep into the formerly unaffected areas of my life.

Trauma tends to be situational, but it's compounding. Even our unresolved childhood trauma can creep up in the most surprising ways. Imagine going about your business, getting your favorite latte from Starbucks, and somebody accidentally takes your drink from the counter.

They may have thought it was theirs, but you knew it was yours, so you lash out. Little did they know that your toys were taken from you when you were kid, and you haven't dealt with it yet. These deep childhood wounds can manifest in our psyche in a million ways if we don't look at the issues, address the needs, and bring solutions. We end up circumnavigating life around the trauma that now defines us. That was a simple but profound example of how it doesn't take much to set us off when we are dealing with unresolved trauma.

It's like building a system of thoughts and actions around an oak tree planted in the middle of our highway. Instead of removing it so we can have free access to travel and do what we want, feel the freedom to engage in any kind of relationship and any opportunity; instead, we choose to slow down and drive around this trauma. Of course, it lends itself to blind spots because we can't see around this tree. Driving around it affects our speed, but sometimes the leaves come down, branches get in our way, and we crash our car. But when you're in trauma, you can't see that there's a tree there. You may think you're in the middle of a clear highway, but you're actually in the middle of a forest.

The difference between someone who goes through a healing process and someone who doesn't is how they respond. Our response is everything. It's actually the only thing that we can control. The situations and events that take place around us are often out of our hands. What else is left to do but to choose how to respond?

Finding healthy coping strategies

If you don't stop to help yourself improve, who will be there for people around you when they need help? Oftentimes, it's our sense of duty that puts us into action. I know this was the case for me. I couldn't let down my kids or my family, so I needed to stop any excuses I may have had immediately. The sense of duty is likely what saved me in this season. If no one needed me as they did, then I'm unsure where I would be. This phenomenon had me back at work just two weeks after Madison died. I needed to be "doing" something, I was going crazy at home. I needed work as a brain break.

Being productive is actually really helpful when you're grieving. Many people find it healing to do something with their hands, like work on something, garden, or build. Some people get a tremendous benefit from returning to work right away, so they can take a break from the emotional toll of their situation and apply themselves to something less burdensome. They're able to see moments of progress.

Not every stage of grieving is supposed to be quick and efficient. Not every trauma is measured the same, because each person is so different. So give yourself some grace if you don't feel like you're progressing fast enough. The goal is to take steps to improve your well-being—mentally, physically, and environmentally—so you can pass that on to those around you.

For your sake and also for those around you, do everything you possibly can to not introduce an unhealthy coping strategy that brings you temporary relief. As much as we want to fix our emotions, feelings, and our depression quickly with alcohol, drugs, and prescriptions, it doesn't always end well. It means that we can't facilitate change and must do it independently without substances to alter our minds. Those inhibitors make us feel better. Will they be able to support us for the rest of our lives without any negative consequences? It's unlikely that we will be able to find the progression and help that we need if we partake in bad coping strategies to feel relief. I'm not saying don't have a glass of wine or a beer; you have your own convictions, but can we agree that you need to work to get yourself to a better place because that alcohol won't do the job? It also goes without saying that many drugs that people take for relief from trauma and loss are addicting, and they will lead to further trauma and loss if they aren't given up. No judgement from me, I definitely indulged in my evening glasses of wine, but today I'm celebrating more than 500 days alcohol-free and I've never felt better.

Acceptance allows us to start healing

Sometimes, what's done is done, and you can't take it back regardless of how much you want to, but sometimes things are redeemable and fixable. If you crash your car, or you break up with someone, there are ways to work those things out. If you lose a loved one like I did, there's no way to bring them back. In all of our considerations, though, we choose to be active participants in our decisions and behaviors going forward. If we're mindfully and emotionally aware, then perhaps with a little help, we can make it through this very difficult time.

We're going to choose to take the next step, and we're not just going to let it happen to us. We're going to choose our next emotion and the behavior that will accompany it, and we're not just going to let our emotions be free anymore. Acceptance is, in essence, a form of responsibility. At a minimum, we're saying to ourselves and those around us that we don't have all the answers, but we're going to agree to a reality in which difficult things can exist, yet they don't control us. It's an empowered state of thinking to realize that we are part of a bigger world we can't fully control.

Whether you believe in God or not, you'll have to invite acceptance into your life. It's often a tension between what we know, what we don't know, and our ability to allow those things that are out of our control a place to exist. The way we do that is to try to find a redemptive purpose for the pain and suffering we've endured. Many people look to their spirituality to accomplish this. Inviting God into this conversation is often useful because it lets us properly position ourselves as a small vessel in this big world. Depending on what kind of acceptance we're willing to participate in, we may find our purpose in the pain we've now experienced, and then finally, we can rebound.

REFUSING THE VICTIM ROLE

Every day, we choose what side of the bed we want to wake up on. We choose what we eat for breakfast and what time we want to go to work. We choose the car we drive. Our life is filled with choices. But what happens when something so crazy, unexpected, and extreme happens to us? We are given a choice, but this time, instead of choosing the inconsequential things, we make a choice about our identity, our core belief systems, our values, and our future. We don't always realize these pivotal moments of life when they happen, but they change our lives in a moment.

Trauma and loss is unmistakably one of those times. It rattles us to the core of who we are, and the foundations of what we know to be true based on our past and future expectations; it has all been upended. There's no way to anchor ourselves anymore. The expectations of what we were planning for, what we hoped for, and what we dreamed for are oftentimes gone. We even question our past because the past didn't help us predict the future; worse, maybe it did. Our lives are put into a spiral of the unknown.

I know what this place feels like, and I'm sure many of you also know how it feels. We physically don't know what's up and down because our minds, emotions, and perspectives are spinning so fast. It's easy to get lost because we no longer know who we are. This is the real effect of trauma. To experience life-altering situations and overwhelming pain is hard to comprehend. As a matter of fact, I don't think our brain comprehends well because it's overwhelmed. It's so much easier to shut down. That's why we want to retreat and sleep when the stress of our moment is too much.

My nanny came back in to help me with my kids during my time of grieving. I needed her. I made deliberate steps to show her and others that I fully supported her. There were a lot of accusations regarding Madison's death. Everyone wants to blame someone. But I didn't blame her at all. I made sure she rode with our immediate family in the limo on the way to the funeral. I had her sit right next to me at the funeral, she stood next to me at the graveside service. I fully supported her and do not blame her for what happened. End of story! I am so grateful that it was her there that day when Madison died. I have played this scenario over and over in my head and I know if it had been anyone else at the house that day, blame would have been on my mind. Because it was Lori, my mind never ever went there. So I asked her to come back and help me with my kids, and she did.

After I lost my daughter, I had a few moments where I laid in bed with my youngest son. I thought that I had every justification for not doing anything that day. My nanny came in and told me to get up. "You can't stay there. You have got to get up." She knew that my physical body had to act out what my mental and emotional state wouldn't. So I got up. Physical movement helped me get through that day. I learned a valuable lesson in this moment.

We all know it's so much easier to just lay in bed, pull the blankets over our heads, and not accept any responsibility for the moment. We may even convince ourselves that the whole world is out to get us and God hates us. I'm sure our imagination will come up with a million reasons why that's true. But what if it isn't? What if optimism and hope define us rather than our situations? Some things in life are difficult, like waking up every day choosing the person that we want to be.

Experiencing trauma and loss is not the same as being a victim. At some point, somewhere in the mindset of our equilibrium, we need to decide who we are. Either before trauma and loss, during it, or afterward. The great distinction between those who get up off the ground when knocked down and those who stay there is their reason why. I always say (and I have a tattoo representing this), "fall down seven times, but stand up eight!" Why we do things, why we care, and how we live, are all based on our mindsets, beliefs, hopes, and dreams. Our resolve is surely tested in times of trauma. In some cases, the test feels like it's too much to handle, and in other cases, our resolve has been proven. Every person's situation is different.

In this chapter, we're going to take back ownership of our own lives to the extent that we're able. When we experience trauma and loss, we need to be able to step back into our shoes and own our moment again. Rather than just letting everything happen to us and accepting defeat, we need to own our next thought, our next decision, and our behavior that surrounds it. It's not easy to do, but what choice do we actually have?

Our minds and emotions will be at war

When trauma hits, the reality of our situation will be questionable. Our minds and our emotions will often be at war with each other. Our mind seeks a logical explanation along the path of least resistance or patterns it's seen in the past. Our emotions are screaming at us, ready to be resolved. Everything that we're feeling is likely to be justified. This may seem like a tornado going through our lives. We look around to see what we can hold on to so we don't lose ourselves. And at this moment, it's pure survival. We're just trying to make it to the next moment. We're not expecting any forward movement, retrospection, or problem solving in front of us. We're just surviving. I did a lot of "just surviving."

Everyone experiences these kinds of situations differently. If you read a book about someone's experience, it will differ from yours. But there are similarities in that we're still human and will experience some of the same patterns just as we did in the grieving process. We need to know that we're not alone in this. As much as we like to convince ourselves that we're totally isolated and no one can relate, there's a world out there that can. You don't have to grieve alone, you don't have to accept your reality alone, and you don't have to plan your future alone; that is a choice. I wish I had realized this earlier on in my grieving process.

I looked around when I got back from the hospital and stared at the faces of my family. I still needed to be a mother, a wife, and a daughter to my parents. I knew my brother still needed me. Even though, at the time, I thought nobody could relate to the pain that I was experiencing, at least they were willing to sympathize with me and see what they could do to help. This sense of purpose and duty helped me through the toughest times. They needed me, and I needed them. Maybe I needed them more than they needed me because if I didn't have a sense of purpose, then I would be in the middle of a tornado, and I can honestly say I have no idea where I would be right now if I weren't anchored in my family and my career.

Tornadoes do pass; they don't last forever, but for those unfortunate few, they leave a pile of destruction behind. The loss and mess that comes with these tornadoes are hard to fathom. But there's a system in place to help people recover after tornadoes. We know that you can't stay in your demolished house forever. Even though you've lost many valuable things, you can't sit in your flooded basement forever. If your entire neighborhood is destroyed, you can't just stay there forever.

I use this physical example to display our emotional and mental state. Once we've gone through a tornado, we must put a recovery process in place. At a minimum, we have to get out of our current mental and emotional state so it doesn't kill us. I'm not sure if you've seen the recovery efforts from a real tornado, but the moment it strikes, survivors are looked for and pulled out of the wreckage, and the cleaning of debris starts. Shortly after the rebuilding phase begins, after all the utilities are checked and new construction begins, it's pretty systematic, and it's actually illegal for people to stay in condemned properties. If we can't physically stay in condemned realities like destroyed property by law, then why would we stay there emotionally and mentally? If we don't move from where we're at, we may die in our current state. Those are the thoughts that were going through my mind when I was laying in bed a few days after I lost my daughter. What kind of mess am I in, and how will I deal with it?

Not allowing the trauma to define us

After experiencing this devastating loss, I often find myself contemplating the meaning of life, the meaning of pain, and the meaning of death. I generally try to find some good in it because why in the hell would we go through something so traumatic and challenging if there wasn't any good in it? Are some things just set out to be evil, and there's no explanation? Understanding is often hard to come by when it comes to pain. Nevertheless, our minds will continue to wander, convincing us of things that may or may not be true, because they are the most straightforward explanations. I need to find a path forward even though I might not have a full explanation. I am always amazed that when I look backwards at the things that have happened to me and then I reflect on where I am now; the path here has required taking the necessary steps, as hard as they are!

Any one of our situations can define us. It can create such a ripple effect in our lives that everything has to operate around that new thing now. It's okay to allow certain things to define us as long as they bring us to a place of health, hope, and redemption. If we become defined by the thing that took place or what happened to us, how are we living according to our true potential while remaining stuck in a mindset of pain, regret, resentment, and loss?

To be honest, I never saw myself as a victim. Not in this, and not in life. The way that I was raised as a child, my behavior and mannerisms came from a family with a military background. My perspective on problems and troubleshooting was more of a "pile driving" of the situation because you probably can't change it. Just get in and figure it out! One thing about me, I will work hard! I never went to college after I graduated high school, and yet I've been able to become a success, at least in my mind. When I graduated, I went right into the workforce. I've been working since I was 16, and have never looked back. So the only way to succeed, in my view, when I was younger and still today, was to work harder than everybody else because I always had it in the back of my mind that everyone was just a little bit smarter than me.

What can you do to perfect your process, other than work harder than others? My work ethic is a component of the decisions I've made. If I encounter a problem, my job is not to sit around and hope and pray that it changes itself. My mentality has been to just confront it head on, bottle the emotion, and work harder and know that if I don't solve this, no one will do it for me. This is what helped me; I'm not saying it's perfect but it's helped me along the way.

This goes into my mindset about being a victim. Never in my life have I said that I was a victim or associated as a victim. There was only one time in my life where someone called me a victim. I couldn't believe it. I was involved in a particular program, and that was a term that people had used to describe me. I have never taken on that label personally. I don't see myself that way. Regardless of the fact if you take on that label is beside the point; if you're actually acting the part, that's what matters.

Most people that are victims in life don't know they're victims. There's a difference between being victimized when something happens to you and actually accepting that as a personal label, as an identity marker.

We've been through a lot, some of us have been through hell and I can attest to that. But somehow we found a way to make it through. Are we a victim of someone else's situation or actions—yes, perhaps. Can somebody go out of their way and try to victimize us? Yes, but we still have a choice if we want to make that situation a lifelong identity for ourselves. See, you can have many experiences in life and those experiences don't necessarily need to define you. For example, you can go water skiing, you can go boating, and you can choose not to become a professional water skier or a professional boater. It may sound like a silly analogy, but our experiences don't necessarily need to become our identity.

So, what is the victim's identity?

A victim identity, or someone that defines themselves as a victim, is not necessarily through external labels, but through their actions. They have decided to treat themselves and the world around them as though they are a victim. Again, this is not just about what they decide to call themselves or whatever narrative they feel; it is purely based on their actions. Anyone can say, "I'm a victim," and you can clearly see in their actions that they've not been victimized by anyone or anything. They're either misunderstanding the term or they're just making it up, but those that act out of victim mentality on a regular basis through their actions and their behaviors not only have a mindset of being a victim but own it as their identity.

I can remember early on when Tyler, my oldest son, was just in middle school having a conversation about this very topic. I said that we still have a responsibility in life. We have to show up and figure out how to be productive members of society, regardless of what we've been through. I know that sounds harsh. It is harsh. The bottom line though, and the tough truth is this—when you go through a loss as significant as ours, its impact on the immediate family is felt forever. For others though, they go to the viewing, they attend the funeral, and they may attend the gathering afterwards. They may come to visit, even a lot initially, but it's not long until they go back to life as normal, and we are left holding the bag. We are still responsible to show up. We do not get to use our loss as a reason or for validation to be less than or irresponsible.

They take on the very thing that may have been disruptive in their life and use it to redefine their existence, and their behavior. They are using it as a label and a shield to act a certain way in order to receive certain kinds of feedback. This forces others to behave a certain way around them. Make no mistake, this is a choice, and that's the hardest part about trauma. There is an association with the trauma and the loss that we can know really well but we need to know it, experience it, and not marry it. I can speak for myself here, I have an association with trauma and loss because of the things that I've been through. I have a choice in the matter, and still I do not have to accept any particular identity as it pertains to my daughter and losing her. I get to choose who I am and the choice is what defines me. The choice that I make in my mind is what forms and shapes my identity. It is not random and happenstance when we choose to make decisions about how we think or how we feel, because it creates the environment and the realities that we live in.

Problems, trauma, loss, and death happen every day, but victims are made in our minds. This isn't to say that we aren't affected by trauma and loss in a significant way; we are. The difference in what I want us to see here is the opportunity to not let other people's actions and even our own actions scar us in a way where we are no longer able to move forward in life. We need to work towards having a good life, being healthy, living long, and loving people. This is what I choose!

I understand that some may have newfound physical limitations based on their trauma and loss. There are things we cannot replace, realities we can not recreate. However, once we've reached the state of acceptance in the grieving process, we can bring ourselves to rebound from where we are, which I will get into in the next chapter. The rebounding is vital because it allows us to create a new equilibrium for our lives. One which does not evolve around our abuser or our trauma or our loss, but rather in what we can do. It helps us evaluate how much control we have over our own situation, how much power we have over our own mind. Rebounding is from a place of power, and the being a victim is from a place of weakness, and whether we choose power or weakness is up to us.

People who are victims in their mindset create environments to perpetuate the cycle of their victimhood. They find friends who are sympathetic to their cause and will reinforce their ideological states rather than their mindsets. The mindsets that we have in life determine the lens through which we see reality. It can be easily understood when you say this person gets me. They understand me. I like them. You like them because something inside of you can agree with who they are and what they're about. In your mind, at the moment, it seems as though they're a better friend because they can relate to you, but perhaps you've selected people who agree with you rather than people who are better for you. Do you see the difference? Our association or blind association with people based on the level of agreement we have with them does not determine health. Health comes from healthy mindsets. We should always ask ourselves why we like a person. Is it because they reinforce positive, wonderful behaviors in our lives, help us accomplish great things, help us move forward in our dreams and aspirations, and love us unconditionally? Those are the positive reasons why we should bring people into our lives, not because they can relate and maintain our painful status.

How do you know if somebody is operating from a victim mentality? Do they repeat the same set of circumstances in the same scenario with no resolve and no ability to move forward? Are they rehashing their pain in a way with different scenarios and different sequences? Here's an example: if someone's spouse cheated on them and they were terribly wounded by that. They have a choice: Do I love again? Do I try to fix this relationship? Do I break off every relationship I've ever had because everyone is bound to repeat the same thing that happened to me? Asking for a friend.

Someone who has a victim mentality would say there's a deep flaw in every person of the opposite sex, and they're all bound to create this exact same scenario for me; therefore, I cannot trust anyone. Do you see how one isolated situation has been reflected onto every person of the opposite sex? That is exactly how the victim mentality starts to progress. Again, this is not to say that the person was not a victim of somebody cheating on them. That was the case, but there is a point where an individual decides that they don't want to perpetuate this reality forever, and, therefore, they're not willing to stay in a permanent state of being taken advantage of. This does not negate that those things occurred; it simply says how one will respond to these scenarios.

Trauma and loss have the ability to change the direction of our lives. They are monumental, they are mountains, they are ginormous events. These events have the ability to affect our spirit, our soul, and our body. There is no mistake in the fact that anybody who has gone through trauma and loss has gone through something significant, something life-changing, and something extraordinary. With that said, trauma and the loss do not need to define you.

Rather, you can use them to assist you. It might seem weird, and it might seem unconventional to try to redirect our pain, but we have a choice, and the choice to remain in our current state or to change is up to us. When we remind ourselves daily of what went wrong and what happened to us—in an emotional and psychological framework, we are reliving our past events, our failures, and our loss. So what does this do to us? It creates a perpetual state of heightened stress and emotion that is unmet and unresolved. If every day I show up and relive the worst moments of my life, it will cause me to react to myself in the world around me in a state of trauma. That trauma, as I've said before, is justified at the moment, but is it justified if I carry that trauma with me in how I think, how I behave, how I act a year later, 5 years later, 10 years later, even 25 years later? The backstop and juxtaposition for this argument would be, what do I have to live for? Am I alive today to relive my past experiences, especially the negative ones? Or am I alive today to make purposeful choices based on my life's outcomes? I know the answer for me!

Assumption of Responsibility

What we decide to live for determines if we will stay in a perpetual state of loss and victimhood or not. So, at some point in my journey, after I've experienced something so significant that it can redefine me, I decide what I want to live for. The decision for me is whether to live with this trauma as my newfound identity, or will I live for myself, my family, my goals, and my aspirations? Am I going to live for my daughter in a way where she would be proud of me, rather than perpetually mourn her loss and blame myself? The reason people can progress from a state of being victimized into not becoming a victim is because they decide what they want to live for. It can be very small. It can be small in the sense that we're deciding to live for life. I'm deciding to live for another person. I'm deciding to live for my goals and aspirations, and I'm deciding to live for God. We choose what we live for, but the greatest thing that we can do for the people that we've lost and the trauma that we've experienced is decide how we can live for them. How we can live for a great cause. How we could live for ourselves rather than deciding how we could live against ourselves, and how we could live against those people that harmed us or let us down.

This may seem, again, unconventional, but the decision lies solely on the basis of responsibility. What are we willing to accept in life, and what we are willing to do. The idea of ownership is interesting. It's also a tough one because if we're in the middle of full-fledged trauma at the operating table in the ER, it's extraordinarily hard to have a conversation with ourselves and the people around us about who's to own this. How do I own this? We aren't able to fully accept ownership until we begin to heal. We have to be pretty much through the grieving stage, or most of its aspects, before we can fully own our situation and start to move forward.

Ownership is not about accepting fault. Ownership is deciding what you will do now and your choices today. Someone who has a victim mindset will say their choices are already made for them. They don't have a choice, which removes all power, influence, and authority from their decision-making abilities. If they do not have a choice, then they are 100% powerless. They're not able to do anything for themselves anymore. If that's the case, the trauma is so significant that it's best that people take care of themselves in their perpetual state 24/7. Unfortunately, this does happen, but if you were not one of those who needed a permanent state of 24/7 care and could make choices for yourself, then you would be able to own the decisions you make today.

Maybe you've just met some new friends, and you've already framed them as the same troublemakers you've experienced in the past. You haven't even allowed them to show that they could be different people, because they're all the same to you. Are you going into every situation with a lens and a mindset of being a perpetual victim, where you haven't even met these new people in a real way but you are already a victim of theirs? It's a mindset, a choice, and a lifestyle. What do you choose?

Ownership invites us on a journey of finding a path forward in life. When we choose to stay in our current state, we refuse to move forward. It may take us a really long time to get to this place of understanding. Have you ever met anyone who experienced a loss and refused to make changes to their loved one's room? They keep the bed sheets the exact same way that they were left. They keep the mess on the floor in the exact same way as when the person was still living. They haven't changed the posters, touched their belongings, or moved the parked car in the driveway. This may seem compassionate, understanding, and loving, and in the moment of trauma, it makes perfect sense, because everything has been shattered.

It is hard to bring the formation of self back to a place of stability, and the search for stability longs for consistency. If one were to change one more item, like moving the dirty T-shirt into the laundry or donating some clothes of someone who passed away, that might bring instability and be jarring. But at some point, there has to be a foundation we can stand on where we can bring those clothes to Goodwill or donate them to a friend, or we can clean the bedroom of the person we lost and sort through their belongings. We can have a funeral, and we can accept the loss for what it is. As hard as it may be, we must accept the loss we've experienced. This is the last stage of grieving, and if we've truly accepted the loss and the trauma, then the only choice left for us is to move forward with our health and life. Before I was even home from the hospital, the dresser that killed my daughter was removed from my house. I still have no idea to this day who exactly removed it or where it went; I just wanted it gone.

The way that we move forward is different for everyone. For me, it was no less than 48 hours after I buried my daughter and the funeral was finished that I was looking at ways in which I could use this situation to better the lives of others. I was researching statistics, how often tip-over accidents happen, etc. I was online researching ways in which furniture can be strapped to the wall, and what can I do about it today. Everybody experiences trauma and loss differently; we're not the same so we're not all going to pivot and jump into action like myself. But I asked myself, can I sit here and do nothing? Can I lie down and just accept defeat? I still had a responsibility that I could not relinquish because the only option I had was to move forward. To move forward with action.

Today is the day

It's nice to have a 24-hour cycle where we can reset. If we have a bad day, we know we can go to bed, wake up the next day, and try again. The process and motion that a 24-hour window brings us is very healing. We know tomorrow will give us a new opportunity that's unavailable today. We should take advantage of time by quarantining our current state today and looking forward to tomorrow. It's the small decisions that we make that define who we are. We can look out on the horizon of our life and say, "all of it's hell and it won't get any better," or we can look into tomorrow and say "I'm hopeful for what tomorrow will bring."

Being a victim is a choice. We can all be victimized by life, but if we choose to remain in that permanent state, then we've accepted a new identity. If we've become a professional victim, the fact is we don't have to stay one. We are the ones who choose this outcome and identity for ourselves. We've probably given ourselves a thousand excuses and a thousand justifications to remain in this current state. But I'm hopeful for those of you who are reading this book and who may identify as victims, that today is the day that ends. You can change and become someone new out of your trauma. You can find a way to move forward. You can find a purpose in your pain if you get out of bed, get dressed, and apply yourself today.

FIRST NAME BASIS WITH THE FUNERAL DIRECTOR

When it rains, it pours. The events preceding the death of my daughter in October of 2007 weren't the end of my trauma. I didn't know that resiliency was being formed in me every day. Unfortunately, the virtue of resiliency comes at a great cost, which I continue to endure. Bear with me as I share the second phase of trauma that I endured after my daughter's passing. I believe some insights and perspectives could be helpful to you as well.

One year and one month later, after my daughter's passing, my twin brother's son Noah, who was four at the time, was diagnosed with stage 4 neuroblastoma. This is an extremely rare childhood cancer. The family decided to start chemotherapy right away. The idea was to try to clean out his marrow enough so that he could maybe have a bone marrow transplant at Duke University.

They started the chemo right away in November, and by the time March came around, the doctor said that his cancer was worse now than when we started. They said there's no way he's going to live. Essentially, anything the doctors do from here on out will be palliative care. This kind of medical care is built around keeping the patient comfortable because no solutions are available. They offered to do some treatments that may prolong his life a little bit, but it was essentially end-of-life care at that moment. Every single hospital in the country wanted to take Noah in for research. They knew they couldn't help him but wanted to research him because his case was so unique. All of the big hospitals with research facilities were happy to take this case on. We knew it wouldn't be for his benefit if he went there. He would not live because of the research, and therefore my brother opted out. The doctors were super clear: the research would not save him, the toll on the family would be high, and the results would not be. It was time to ensure that the quality of Noah's remaining life would be epic.

Noah was immediately placed on top of the Make-A-Wish Foundation's list. Make-A-Wish was prompt, and they sent Noah to Disney because the doctor said he was not going to live through the summer. He did, in fact, live through the summer, which was a blessing. He got to do everything that he wanted to do, like go see Thomas the Train in Baltimore. He wanted to go to his first day of kindergarten, and he was able to. Anything his 4-year-old brain could come up with, we did our best to see if we could make it happen. One could say he lived his very best life.

It was soon after the start of kindergarten when Noah started to deteriorate significantly, and he died one year and one day after his original diagnosis. November, 2009. It's weird to process his death because I feel like I struggled harder with his passing than my daughter's. The rationale behind my feelings is that when my daughter passed away, I was able to find purpose. Her heart valves were donated to two kids in need, and the blood that flows through those kids' bodies is done so with the assistance of my daughter's contribution. She also donated many other things, like tissue. Maddie's Message is also helping save lives by educating families on furniture tip-overs. So when I look at my daughter's contribution to the world around her, I see that her life has continued to have meaning, and our loss wasn't in vain—good came out of it. This is something that I've been thinking about for some time.

Now with Noah, of course his diagnosis and passing were unexpected and extremely hard for the family, just as my daughter's was, but when you have cancer, you can't donate any of your organs. I've struggled to see the redemptive side of this loss. It just feels wrong. What good came out of this? I can't wrap my mind around it. It's not just puzzling. It's troubling. It just feels like unmatched trauma and pain with no answer and no purpose. It just feels evil. How could God let this happen? No 5-year-old should die of cancer. No little boy should wake up one day blind. He suffered more than he should have. I didn't understand why. I will remember calling the funeral home, preparing for the inevitable with Noah. Trying to understand the logistics of what would happen after he passed. It was then that the funeral director said "It's bad, Carri, that I'm starting to recognize your voice." For me, I never thought I'd be on a first name basis with Walt, the funeral director. But here we are, and it still wasn't over.

The emotional toll and struggle were real for me. My twin brother and I were pretty much the opposite version of each other. I always thought the best of him, but I knew he couldn't make the best life decisions. I'm thinking to myself, how will he deal with this? I know he's married, but their relationship was questionable at times. My bald-headed, 270 lb 6 ft 1 brother would always say I got the looks, and you got the brains. But I genuinely thought there's no way he's capable of handling this loss in a real, meaningful way. His son was his whole entire world. I just did my best to try and support him alongside my parents, and be there for him by helping out with some of the funeral arrangements and just being present. I worried about how he would function. We were twins, but I always took care of my brother. I had no idea we'd both be mourning the loss of our children. A daughter for me, and a son for him.

6 weeks later

So we buried Noah in November of 2009, and six weeks later, in January, my brother went into the emergency room not feeling well. He told the ER doctors that he couldn't breathe. Of course he can't breathe because he hasn't taken care of himself in the past year and a half. He's been working three jobs to try to make ends meet and take care of his son's expenses, and his wife was a piece of shit—she was the least supportive person around. Criminal even. The thing is, I tried hard to give her grace. She lost a son for God's sake. But at every turn though, she made bad decision after bad decision. We found out that she had taken out a fake life insurance policy on her son. When it was time to pay for the funeral, there was no actual money. My brother had believed everything she told him. It was hard.

In early January of 2010, my brother received a diagnosis of stage 4 lung cancer, and they wanted to do surgery on him right away. It didn't look good. His entire left lung was basically a tumor. Initially he wasn't even going to get treated. He knew what cancer treatments looked like, his son's journey was still fresh in his mind. I was with him in the room when he asked the doctor how much time he had if he chose to do nothing and just live a quality life. The doctor responded that he only had three months to live. This information was hard to wrap our brains around.

We opted for chemo and radiation, and we started immediately. Initially the doctors did not recommend surgery to remove the cancer, but after three weeks of radiation he was responding like a champ. They changed their mind and now surgery was on the table as a viable option. His wife didn't want him to have the surgery, even though the doctor said he was going to die if he didn't have it. So either don't have the surgery and die, or have the surgery and there is a chance to live. He wanted the surgery, but his wife didn't want him to have it. Can you believe that? I know that she understood that if he lived, she would end up being his caretaker, and she was not interested in that life for herself. It was pitiful and sad to watch. I clearly have no love lost for that woman.

He ended up having the surgery and they removed the left side of his lung, as well as a golf ball sized tumor from his heart ... AND he survived! He survived the surgery, it was a miracle. It was really questionable whether or not he would make it through, but he persevered. I'll spare you all of the crazy details, but as you might guess, during the early stages of his recovery, while he was still in the hospital, his wife came in and asked for a divorce. Who asks for a divorce when your husband is dying of cancer? I can tell you who, someone who in that moment thought that my brother had beaten cancer, and that was now going to require a lot of care from her. As soon as he was in the hospital and he stopped making money, she knew that her whole lifestyle was going to change because he couldn't work three jobs anymore. That's how I know she's a piece of shit.

So immediately, I stepped in even more to help because who else would he turn to besides me and his parents? I'm his twin sister. I had always taken care of him, and now would be no different. When he was in the rehab facility, I'd go there and help him, give him haircuts, pedicures, you name it. He didn't have anybody to do that for him. Things were looking promising. One thing I noticed was how he was moving his left arm. Like he was in pain, like it was sore. He started complaining about his arm more and more. He would move it around a bunch, and it was clearly bothering him. We'd massage his arm and see what we could do to help him, but he just kept complaining, saying that it hurt. They x-rayed his arm, and they found a tumor that went the length of his arm, elbow to wrist. I asked the doctor how my brother had lung cancer in his arm. The lung cancer was actually sarcoma, cancer of the tissue. The cancer that we thought was gone, has spread throughout his body. They found spots in his arm and on his back. This was not the news we expected. We knew and still know God's timing is perfect, but in this moment, that was very hard to understand. Why go through all of this just to still end up in the same place, knocking on death's door.

The doctors would radiate the spots they found, which reduced their size and relieved some of the pain. But the doctor said there's nothing really we can do with sarcoma. It's already spreading. And he looked at me and said, "What do I do now? I've lost my son, this week I lost my wife, I've lost everything. I don't want any more cancer treatments. I saw what they did to my son. I'm not doing anything else. Whatever life I have left, I just want to have my best life."

We went right to work arranging hospice care at my parent's home in Virginia Beach. We were all set to have the ambulance transfer him from Wake Forest Baptist in Winston Salem to Virginia Beach. The morning of the transfer, I got a call from the doctor. I was so scared she was going to say my brother had died, but what she said was that he had complained of a headache, so they scanned his brain. They found more than 20 lesions in his brain. I asked what this meant. The doctor wanted to do brain radiation before transferring my brother home. He again asked for my advice, and I responded with no. I said you can talk, you can smell, you can hear, you can taste, you can feel. As soon as they start doing radiation on your brain, you might lose some, if not all, those functions. Right now, I can sit here and have a conversation with you, but after radiation, I might not be able to. No more treatments, no messing with your brain. Let's focus on living your life fully, whatever time we have left—so that is what we did. The date was April 9, 2010. The doctor told me that my brother had a week to live, maybe two, but that he won't last a month. He arrived home to my parents' house that night. He would live his best life for the next several days, surrounded by family and friends, and most importantly by unconditional love. I can honestly say that during that period of time, he probably felt the most love that he's ever experienced in his life.

When we left the hospital, I knew I had to take some steps to protect him, the way I always had. I took the necessary steps to become his full caretaker and assumed power of attorney over his affairs, at his request. I took care of my brother until the day he died.

Once settled in at home with my parents, my dad gave him a bell and said ring this once if you need your mom, and ring it twice if you need Aunt Diane. My mother was a retired nurse, so she was able to help take care of him, which was amazing. Aunt Diane is my mom's best friend, and also a nurse. They were there to help and provide different shifts of care. He was surrounded by the best care any patient could ask for. So my mom was #1, Diane was #2 and my dad was #3. Three rings if you need dad. One time my brother rang three times, and my dad didn't come. He said, "I thought you just wanted your mom and Aunt Diane together." (1+2=3) This was a joke; we all got a good laugh out of that.

It was hard sitting there trying to be an emotional support for him when nobody else could do it. I mean, really, his parents were going through tremendous trauma. They were doing their very best. They lost their granddaughter, and then just lost their grandson a few months earlier, and now their son is dying of cancer and is given less than 30 days to live. They were neck deep in a crazy amount of trauma. I think it feels different when you lose one of your kids. I'm still trying to process the pain of the last two losses. One of the things that was especially hard was some of the last conversations I had with him.

He can still maintain a good conversation even though he is immobile in many ways. He'd say stuff like, "We're going to hit the golf course soon, right?" We initially started playing along, but then we realized that maybe he didn't know that he was going to die. My parents were concerned that he didn't know he was going to die, and that was something really important for him to process. I said I'm positive he knows he's going to die.

Nevertheless, my parents asked me to talk to him. So I did. My parents went to church that Sunday, and I went over to talk to him.

"Hey, what do you think about all this? I asked. "

"What do you mean?"

"Well, do you know you're getting ready to die?"

"Yeah."

"The doctor said you had one week, maybe two, but you weren't going to live a month. Do you remember him saying that?"

"Yeah, okay."

"Well, we're at the two-week mark, and so it's really any moment now. You may just close your eyes and not wake up. So what do you think about that?"

"Don't think about it. I don't want to.".

But then he asked me what I thought about it.

I told him when Madison died, I was able to wrap my brain around the fact that she's an organ donor and she saved lives. It sucks, but I found purpose there. When your son died, I couldn't find any purpose there, and that really broke my heart for you, and I've struggled with that. I can't understand it. It's hard to explain that to my kids. So here we are less than six months after you buried your child, and at any moment, you're going to close your eyes and go to Heaven. If you are comforted knowing that Noah will be there when you arrive, then it makes sense to me. You get to see your son, whom you love so much. It makes sense that you go early to see him. I know that's the only thing you truly cared about on this Earth. He nodded in agreement. I knew he knew. He was at peace.

I told him that when he went to Heaven, he should send me back a message and tell me that he was okay. I said I want you to tell me that Noah and Maddie are okay. He said sure, what should it be? I said how about things in twos? Because we're twins. Maybe when I see things in twos, you will tell me everything's okay. It will be our little sign, We agreed. He confirmed that he knew he was going to die and that he was going to Heaven. He wasn't so scared anymore and was excited to see his son. Even though we had these difficult conversations, which were very helpful, he would still tease me just as he always did. We had some funny moments in his last days. He had asked me to shave his head—he always keeps his bald, like Mr. Clean bald. He said, "You've got to help me shave my head. I know there's fuzz up there, and I need my head shaved." I told him I'd do it next time I was here.

We always tried to bring in humor during this really difficult time because it helped so much. Of course, my mom was willing to make him anything he wanted to eat, so sometimes I was like, 'ask for this, or ask for that'… and he would. He would say you need to tell her what we want, and then tell her what I want to eat afterward. Humor seems to split the air in the room. I could tell he was in a lot of pain. So I'd reach for the morphine button, and I'd hit it a few extra times. And he would tell me to stop pushing the morphine button.. I told him I didn't want him to be in pain. We bantered back and forth. I said, "You don't fuss with me because, guess what? When you die, I get to choose whatever you're going to wear to your funeral and I will put you in a Steelers jersey." That was a running joke because he was a die-hard Miami Dolphins fan. "How terrible would that be if you get laid to rest in a Steelers jersey?" And he would tell me to not bury him in a Steelers jersey—that would be the worst thing that could possibly happen.

We continued this routine for the next week, and my mom watched him. May 2nd, I got a phone call from my mom and she said that he had a seizure. I knew this meant the ending was close. He could no longer talk to us, although he could respond by squeezing our hands. On Tuesday morning, I was headed over to the house, and I called and I asked my mom if she wanted a smoothie since I was swinging by Tropical Smoothie on my way over. She said that she was making my brother breakfast. which was a surprise because when he had that seizure he had not talked or communicated for a couple of days.

"What do you mean you're making him breakfast?" I asked.

"I walked downstairs today, and he said, 'Mom, can you make me some oatmeal?' It's incredible that he just kind of woke up."

This was coming up close to my mom's and my sons' birthdays, May 5 and May 6. I said to myself I hope he doesn't die on one of their birthdays. Tyler was especially close to his uncle, and I didn't want him to have to live with that. I know it sounded selfish, but I just didn't want to ruin it for those birthdays forever. The 5th came and went, and we celebrated with my mom, the 6th also came and went.

When I got to the house I was teasing him and I said, "What are you doing? You think you can have a little seizure, scare us like that, not talk for a few days, and then just wake up this morning wanting breakfast?" We laughed! He said, "You told me you were going to shave my head, and you haven't shaved my head yet." He really wanted his head shaved. I was like, let me get on that right now, and I lathered him up and shaved his bald head. He couldn't lift his hands to his head, so I lifted them for him so he could feel it and confirm that I did a good enough job. I asked him if that felt good. He said, "I guess you did okay." It would be my final chance to take care of my brother the way I always had. Eddie lived that day but had a seizure that night; he never regained the ability to speak, and at noon on Mother's Day, May 9, 2010, he went to Heaven.

Things in twos

He died on a Sunday, we buried him on Wednesday, and on Friday I was at the bank drive-through and I just happened to look up—I saw two white butterflies dancing in sync. I felt like it was a hug from heaven. That's what we agreed on, things in twos. I felt comforted then and said to myself, I didn't need anything else. I know that he's in Heaven with Maddie and Noah, and I felt completely at peace.

After that moment, I sought to see the significance of the timing of everything. When I reached out to the funeral director to talk about my brother's passing, I asked them if the bill for Noah had been paid. They said none of the bill was paid. So I took the life insurance policy that my brother had in place, and I paid off Noah's funeral bill, and then I said I don't want to leave here with a cent. I want to make sure that everything that he needs is taken care of. If you've ever had to go through the process of planning a funeral, you know there is a long sheet that you have to fill out, making determinations and decisions about what to have, type of casket, flowers, limos, preachers, music, etc. At the end of the day, there was just enough money. So, in a beautiful way, my brother did get to pay for his son's funeral as well his own, and I found that redemptive.

Even though I experienced trauma after trauma, and it felt like it was never-ending, I also saw some beauty in between those hard moments, if that makes sense. Slowly but surely, I felt like there were some redeemable moments that were taking place during trauma and after trauma. I was open to anything but felt like I was getting a little love from these helpful moments.

Going back to the year that Maddie died in October. I always told myself our little family was not complete. I still wanted another baby and would keep trying until I had a girl. Maddie died in October, and I was pregnant again with a girl in December of 2007. Ellie was born in August of 2008; she's now 17 years old, and I can't imagine my life without her. In some weird way, I know it's by design, because if I didn't lose Maddie, I might not have had Ellie. That's a strange thought because I'm looking at my 17-year-old now. I've been able to live my life with this wonderful soul, and I wouldn't trade her life for anything. So maybe this is God's perfect way of sorting things out because surely my mind can't comprehend all of it. We might not understand everything that happens to us, but if we can stay engaged and not quit, then resilience will take over, and hopefully, we'll end up with something good on the other side, just like I have.

REBOUND

There's a time for rebounding after we've accepted the loss and the trauma that we've experienced. We're now getting the opportunity to gather our thoughts, values, and actions. We assess the damage that has ensued and determine what can be salvaged, what can be fixed, and what's left. I'm not only talking about the physical damage, but the emotional damage, damage to our reputation, our image, and our identity. Every single thing is tested when we experience significant trauma. One moment, we fully trust ourselves to make good decisions, and the next moment, after trauma, we don't trust ourselves at all. One moment before trauma, we love and support specific individuals, and then after trauma, we can't look at them. In the rebounding phase, we take inventory of who we are, what we're about, and what our core belief systems are. Then, through this framework, we establish our value systems and behaviors.

If we're currently experiencing trauma then we probably don't want to establish new belief systems around that trauma because it will be reactionary. It will be like the oak tree that we talked about earlier. We will live our lives pretending that this obstacle does not exist, even though it does, and it affects us every day. We need to be in a good place in our grieving to begin to rebound. If we've not reached levels of acceptance within ourselves, then we're not rebounding anything because rebounding is also rebuilding.

Can we rebound when we are in pain? The answer is yes. The reality of our situation is that one example of pain may come up now, and we have another example tomorrow. Just because one situation is resolved in one form or another doesn't mean we won't have another situation to deal with. This is the same thing that happened to me. I had one experience of loss and trauma and then two more right after it. The goal is not to find a way out of the pain. The goal is to try to find a purpose in the pain. Throughout the following chapters, we will look at a process allowing us to repurpose our pain.

Rebounding for ourselves first

I'm open to admit that one of the hardest things that I've experienced throughout this trauma is trying to figure it out on my own. Perhaps my stubbornness and my propensities have made my healing from trauma a solo journey. I also find strength in my process because I have dealt with several life-changing situations, and I'm still standing. However, I know how important it is to look back at rebounding for ourselves first. Before I begin to consider my kids, my spouse, my dog, or any of my friends, I need to put a plan in place for my sanity. I need to be able to sort through my pain, my thoughts, and my emotions in a way that progresses my life in a positive direction. As the flight attendants tell us when we are flying, if the oxygen masks drop, put your own on first before you try to help others. How profound is that. We can't be there for others if we have not taken care of ourselves. Man, I wish I had understood that so long ago.

I never got the help I needed. I had three children who needed me, two of which had suffered several losses at such a young age. I was determined to help them, at all costs. I did the best I knew how to do.

But what I mean is that I never felt held by others; I always felt I had to take care of myself. I take full responsibility for that. I'm sure I felt unhelpable to them, like I had it all together. I'm not mad about it, but it's a fact, and I had to deal with it. So, I've taken a solo approach to getting help, and honestly, most of what I picked up has just been through the years of grinding it out. I didn't stop and actually have a season to go through self-mastery and healing, and then come out the other side like an Eat, Pray, Love epiphany. Sometimes, I feel like I am the clown at a rodeo, and nobody has told me to get out of the way. But somehow, I survived—and looking back now, I try to find ways to improve myself continuously.

I realized that if I have to depend on myself significantly, which I do, I need to continue to pour into myself. There are podcasts and music that I listen to that have changed my life, and books that I've read that have altered my heart and my mind. Some find tremendous value in gleaning from the wisdom and guidance of others on a regular basis. I encourage you to do so if you can't stop everything and get a holistic season to yourself. The Casting Crowns were on repeat in my early grieving days, as well as Steven Curtis Chapman. "Praise you in this Storm" was my mantra for so long, trying to keep present to the fact that there is only a plan A. What can I learn from this storm? How can I use this trial to help others, and myself? When SCC came out with his album *Beauty Will Rise* after the death of his little girl, the words resonated deeply with me. I believe "out of these ashes, beauty will rise." I experience glimpses of this still today.

Maybe my internalized process has slowed down the growth that I may have seen, but I did the best with what I had, given the situation. That's why people read books like these: they can prevent slow progression if they can pick up the keys in wisdom beforehand. That's what I hope for you in this. I may have avoided pain and trauma if I got help sooner, but hindsight is always 20/20. I hope to be your hindsight today.

Who do you talk to when you can't trust yourself?

I remember going to work one day right after we lost Maddie, and my company came to me and said, you know, we've been providing counselors and therapy to the people underneath you because this trauma has affected you so much that it's affected them. I didn't even realize how much I projected my world onto others. My employees needed to see counseling and therapy. That's wild. It's not wild that they needed therapy. It's wild that my world was spilling over into theirs so much that they needed help dealing with my trauma.

This was eye-opening for me; I knew I wanted to help my employees and ensure they got the chance to talk to counselors and therapists. I was trying to deal with it myself. I know I was fumbling through the process, trying to keep everything going, and I wasn't really taking time for myself. One of my regrets is that I didn't see enough value early on in getting help for myself. I didn't want to project myself as weak or someone who needed something. I tried to be strong, and in some ways, that's taking a toll on me, and I've over-compensated in other areas. Looking back, I would have jumped into more counseling and therapy early on. It would have given me one or two things each week to build onto so I could feel more supported when I had the greatest need.

I think it's important for us to seek expert guidance and help when we're experiencing trauma. Not only do professionals have a path and a plan that they've learned and practiced with many others, but they're not in our current situation. Their minds are not clouded with a mixture of pain and emotion. They can see above our situation and help us out of it or through it.

I remember when my pastor spoke to my ex-husband in the emergency room and said, "You're not going to be able to rely on each other in this next season. You'll need to devote time and energy to healing, but your spouse might not be there for you because they're healing." This was important to hear because I felt free, and I've always been the one people lean on and get support from. At that moment, I had permission to devote more time and energy to myself outside of caring for my family. It was also helpful to know that the swirl of emotion and the difficulty of the situation required help from others. From the moment of my loss, I received help from the assistance at work, the police who showed up, the fire trucks and the ambulance, the ER staff and the doctors, and the donor programs. All these people had skill sets, and they utilized them to help me. When we're in need, we need to rely on others that are not at the same place that we currently are at right now but they can expertly and professionally guide us to a better place. You may have to rebuild.

Trauma, pain, loss—they don't care about the expectations and plans that you had. It's like analyzing a demolition site. You got to walk around and see what pieces are still around. What's left standing? You're going to do this for yourself, for your identity, can you trust yourself again, can you love yourself again? You'll also need to analyze what remains of your family construct. The family construct that you had before is not the same now; there's a big fracture in the middle of your living room that you might not be able to cross. Trauma creates extracurricular conflict, especially among family members and spouses. This, I found out very quickly. It's hard to recover from the loss of a child, and in my case, my marriage to Wally could not make it through this hurdle. The trauma and loss alone brings division without any words spoken. In addition to that, we add our emotions and frustration, resentment, pain, and trauma back into the relationship that we once had. It was a slow fade. I'm grateful for the father Wally is to our children, and the person he is today, and I grieved the loss of this marriage long before physically separating and divorcing.

As a parent who has experienced loss, we tend to take care of ourselves last. You know how it goes: kids get fed first, the kids need to go first in everything, and then you take care of yourself with whatever energy and time you have left. I needed to reassess my relationships with each one of my kids and establish care and a new value system with them. Of course, I didn't want to lose them, but I wanted this experience somehow to allow us to come together and be closer to one another. Most of the time, we don't do this assessment consciously but internalize small changes we want to make to improve our relationships. The way we go about this is very important, though, because if we're not healthy and we're still in trauma, then we're not improving those relationships—we're making them worse.

I knew I needed to rebuild my relationships when my marriage broke down. Of course, I made a million mistakes, and I could easily blame myself for the rest of my life for those mistakes, but at some point, I needed to own them and move on.

Excuses and justifications keep us from building the new life we want. I'd be the first to say that I could give you a million excuses and justifications for why I shouldn't be where I'm at right now, but we've got to be able to see light at the end of the tunnel. We have to embrace a reality that takes our life situations and turns them into a useful purpose. We get there by implementing baby steps on the path of healing, connectedness with one another, looking back at our past in a redemptive manner, and taking bold actions that course correct our lives.

I didn't see any change in how I felt, my hope in life, or my outlook when I stayed on the couch. Soon after we buried Maddie, I went to work to see how much good could come of such a tremendous loss. I tried my best to use it as a catalyst to make me a better person and to help and inspire those around us in various ways.

Not off limits

I realized that I needed to establish a few things to help me find stability amid this chaos. For me, we instituted some tiny things that helped us get back on our feet. You may have a different set of ideas and motivations. Maddie and her life are not off limits. This is one of the first things I told my family. I will bring her up in conversation almost daily, and we can discuss her. We get to relive her experiences. Her life is not off limits. This might be foreign territory for a Western culture to embrace. It's often seen as a shameful and hard-to-talk-about process when you speak about someone who's passed away in Western society. In Eastern cultures, they view the loss of a loved one as a different thing. For me, it was purely about not allowing anything to keep us from including her in our family. This was freeing and allowed us to process painful, difficult conversations normally. If someone in the family were having a hard time processing Maddie's loss, we would talk about it. This allowed us to have more of a grounded approach about discussing Maddie.

We also participated in regular visits to her grave. I have to be honest; it hasn't always been easy. It's a difficult place for me to go to. I actually hate it. I'm very grateful for my friend, Erica, who helps me take care of her grave. She makes sure to arrange seasonal bouquets and keeps her headstone looking fresh and cared for.

Because I've made it intentional not to make Maddie's life off limits to my family, and to discuss her, it has positioned me to talk about her and her message anywhere I go. Sometimes, I'm in the grocery store line and want to tell people about Maddie's Message. I get asked to speak at conferences, and I'm happy to share that as well. It is also so beautiful to see my granddaughters, Ava and Aria, speak so clearly about Maddie and how they tell people to anchor their furniture to the walls. She shows up in conversation every single time we see a white butterfly. The girls will say, "There goes Maddie."

This posture is excellent for my family to be open to discussing her. At first we were all processing pain and sometimes we still do but now most of our external processing is based on all the good. Either we're thinking back about what she would be doing or saying, or what good is coming out of her message. It would be tough if we only processed Maddie's trauma all the time. So I'm glad that we healed through that season and were able to process the good now, but we do need to watch over the conversations we have about her to protect it and ensure that it's creating impactful memories for those around us.

Oftentimes, I find myself sharing Maddie's story with another person for the first time, and I end up consoling them for the feelings they are feeling. This is natural, but I also need to remind myself, and sometimes remind them, that I'm not physically in trauma right now, and they don't need to be either. This type of processing is very grounding because I can talk about her and share her message anywhere and everywhere I go. I know it affects people, but I'm not immobilized to speak about her because it's difficult anymore. Rather, I embrace complex subjects and conversations. It didn't take long before people started calling me the death expert. I frequently get a phone call from someone who just lost somebody or knows of someone who did. They ask me how to handle it, what should they say, how should they act. It's not something I had on my bingo card, but I am happy to fulfill the role as long as I need to.

Support networks

It's not wise to rebound alone, especially after you've been through such significant trauma. Several groups were beneficial to me in my time of need. Through Facebook, I found a group of people who have experienced the same loss as me. The people in the group had all experienced losses from furniture tip-overs. It was comforting for me to find them and to be a part of this group—they understood the loss and the pain that I went through. We call ourselves PAT (Parent's Against Tip-Overs). We could relate on the emotional front, and it was very connecting and rewarding to talk about ways in which we could help educate other parents. Processing our pain with others is healing because we feel known, supported, and loved. We have accomplished a lot together, notably getting the STURDY Act passed into law in December of 2022.

Life Net Health is probably one of the most significant resources for me. Not only was I in touch with them from the beginning as a donor mom, but then eventually as a grief companion. They have been a consistent connection for me through the years. Grief companions—generally, how it goes is if you have a child that dies and their organs are donated, you're put in touch with someone who also had that happen to them. You get to talk to a parent who had to process a similar situation. Of course, they're trained to walk you through the grieving process, and they will be there as your grieving companion to the extent that you need them and want them to help you. This is a lifeline for some people because someone knows how they feel, knows the experience they just went through, walks them through the other side, and helps them rebound. About 18 months after Madison died, I went through the training program to be a grief companion for others. This was helpful for me because I could use my experience and understanding to help another person, just as Madison helped another by donating her organs. I am still a grief companion, currently walking this journey with three other grieving mothers.

I had to reassess some of my closer friendships because their voices were not speaking health and positivity into my healing journey. They cared more about their opinions than they did about my growth and inability to rebound. As hard as it is to say this, we have to be able to set boundaries and not listen to those who are not helping us, regardless of how close they may have been to us in past seasons. Trauma affects people tremendously, and every step we make into rebounding our lives may not be the same caliber or growth that those around us are making. That's why we need to analyze our journey and not allow the journeys of others to derail us or hold us back.

You may be thinking, *oh, it's fine. I'll keep the same people in my life; they can say whatever they want, and I won't be affected by it.* But what if you are kept in a painful state of trauma for 15 or 20 years because you listened to the wrong people, continuously? Do you see how negative interactions can permeate your mind and your heart into inaction and more trauma? It's a fallacy to think that those who have been around you the longest will benefit you most in a season of need. Sometimes, this is the case because they know and love us the best; however, it's not always true. That's why we need to be able to rebound into what we hope and dream about for our situations. If we can't see the light at the end of the tunnel, then what are we doing all of this for?

If we find the wrong people to grieve with, perhaps people in the same victim stage that we are in, then there's a chance that they've been there for a while, and what we might get out of that relationship is more of the same. Respectfully, just because someone's gone through trauma, doesn't mean that they have the skills to help you out of yours. Some people have committed to enduring their suffering and are so prideful. Their ego is so set on maintaining this perfect imbalance that people feel the need to help them because they're always victims. Lots of narcissistic people, and those who have narcissistic tendencies, take on a victim persona because it serves their ultimate image. Surround yourself with people who can push you forward and not keep you where you are.

Some people that I'm close to have spoken very negatively to me and made the healing difficult to process. Their 'word vomit' makes it all the more difficult to heal and overcome, because now if you disagree with them, there could be a relational conflict in addition to the trauma that just ensued. It's okay to have boundaries; tell them no. Tell them to keep their thoughts to themselves if they can't help you with what you are building. Everyone's opinions are their own. Everyone's process is their own. We all rebound differently. So when we bring ourselves into someone else's world, we must come in as sporting, loving, and accepting. We have to own our part and allow others to own theirs.

Closure

Rebounding takes closure. If we don't see closure through our grieving process, and acceptance of some of our actions, then we can't move on. Shortly after I buried my daughter, the investigation concluded into our potential involvement in her death. Of course, we were cleared and found not guilty of any wrongdoing. The detectives closed the case and didn't need to interrogate our family anymore. Although we knew we wouldn't be held criminally liable, it helped us to see the closure of this investigation. I guess, in a way, we couldn't move forward without it. Its closure was a requirement for us to be able to start healing.

In the same regard, I also saw closure and some of my failed expectations. I needed to let go of the possibility of having Maddie in our lives in the physical sense anymore. I needed to go to a funeral and walk through that process physically. The interesting thing about funerals is that they're not for the person who passed away, but for the people in attendance. We all need to see and feel the closure of these traumatic moments. Physically being there at the funeral allowed us to go through a process together that brought closure. I remember so clearly the Pastor sharing that on the day Madison died, on that very Tuesday, God was not having an off day. This accident did not catch him by surprise. Madison was supposed to live for 757 days and that is exactly what she did. She
is in Heaven, perfect. Not to be unkind, but Madison is not missing us here on Earth—we are missing her though. These remarks by our Pastor provided a comfort that I can't explain. Knowing this was part of his plan has helped my healing, even though I'd want her back in a second if I could reverse time.

So, rank and file, I went through the feelings and expectations I had through the years and saw closure for those that are no longer possible. This didn't all happen at once. As a matter of fact, I still do it today. But I'm open to confronting closure because I know it's essential for my well-being. If I'm not willing to close an expectation or an emotion, then what good will it bring me? Another example of closure is getting the news on February 13, 2008 that Maddie's organs were finally ready to be placed. Four months after she died, two other children would live. What a wonderful Valentine's Day gift for those families, heart valves.

Unfortunately, trauma has its relational casualties as well. Sometimes, we can avoid them, and sometimes, we can't. In this case, I lost my husband through this process. We knew that this was a possibility; we talked about it immediately. Marriages tend to not work out after significant loss. We were no different even though we thought we would be. It was a slow fade, as I've mentioned before. No fighting, no yelling, just a slow fade away from each other. Losing lifelong friendships is hard to process, but the separation of your spouse is an extraordinary feat. It has so many areas of connectivity and expectation that it requires a separate grieving process. Not only does it involve every aspect of your life, but it also involves your future hopes and dreams, and in my case, it also involves kids. Looking back now, I think some things are bound to happen, and sometimes we can't control them, so it is what it is, and we have to move on. That doesn't mean we didn't try with everything in us to make it work, but at some point, you have to let people go so they can find their direction, and you can find yours.

When you're in the storm

When we're in the middle of the storm, we often look to our right and to our left to see what we can hold on to. Have you ever seen the movie called *Twister*, where they survive the tornado in the middle of the field by just hanging on? That's how it is sometimes. Some seasons are about survival and picking up the pieces. It doesn't mean it's going to be easy but we just have to make it through until the next day. The way I did that was, subconsciously, I tapped into the rhythm in a cadence with music that fed my soul and quieted my mind. I would listen to Steven Curtis Chapman on repeat with the song called "Beauty Will Rise." I would also listen to Casting Crowns, "I Will Praise You in This Storm." The two songs not only spoke to my heart in terms of the present conflict that I felt, but instilled within me hope that things could get better. I understand that practically didn't make much sense but my belief was set on rebounding. I feel like I am a part of something bigger when I sing and when I listen to these pivotal songs and a difficult season.

I guess I had a choice in ways that I could feed my soul and my mind, and I chose something that could not only relate to my pain but also give me a healthy dose of hope and optimism to bring me out of it. Some people find music that relates to their pain but it doesn't give them an option to grow out of it or redirect it. When we are knee deep in the throngs of life, sometimes we need to find something that we can hold on to. For me, it was God, it was my family, and my belief in the future. I knew if I made it through today then maybe tomorrow will be better. What or who do you hold on to when you encounter trauma and loss?

How will you rebound?

After we have gathered the pieces of our past and formulated the person we want to become, we can put together a plan of action to rebound. But before we can make any actionable change, we must see where we're going. Rather than looking back at what could have been or what should have been, we look forward to the hope of who we are—not the situations that troubled us, but the ones we have an active role in now. I'm talking about our present moment.

Right now, one of our most significant opportunities is to be empowered in our present moment just enough to create an actionable change. We're not thinking and obsessing over the past, and we're not getting depressed over our failed expectations, but we've gathered ourselves just enough to take a baby step in the right direction. Even though our emotions may be telling us to stay hidden, we need to start moving again. Because if we don't, then we will be paralyzed by the analysis of what we don't know, and we will never see the change that we hope to see, or become the person that we hope to be.

Who will you become through this? Most people cannot formulate an exact answer, and that's fine. The best thing we can do is make a small incremental change in the right direction. For me, I had determined in my heart that Maddie's life was not going to be in vain, and I was going to bring about so much good through the loss I experienced, because her life had so much value. People worldwide will know about Maddie's Message, which will help them. I rebounded, one baby step at a time.

REFLECT

In a way, our thoughts are what really make us; they form our identities and define who we are. I can remember countless times standing over my daughter's grave, and I look to the right, and I see my nephew's grave and my brother's grave. It's quiet here; perhaps I can hear a little wind wrestling the leaves and the landscape guy in the distance, but that becomes white noise. I'm left alone here with my untamed thoughts, and boy, do they run wild sometimes. My mind can run in 12 directions at once, and in a matter of a minute, I can relive my past and all my failures and punish myself for all the things that I've done wrong to bring this about—or I can look into my past and reflect on what good will come of this. The choice is really up to me; one is way more destructive than the other. Something good may come out of my reflections.

Our past considerations either make us or break us. This goes for our heart, curiosities and our minds. We are the gatekeepers of our current and future reality by what we let into our minds and hearts. The power of reflection is not just looking back; it's repositioning ourselves to have a healthy relationship with our past. It's a tool to help us understand where we are in the context of our past, allowing us to utilize it to benefit our future.

Our mindsets are everything

Through the years, I've been insecure for various reasons, and that's a lens through which I've seen the world. As much as I don't want to admit it, my life has been affected by my mindset and feelings of insecurity. It's like waking up every day and putting on glasses, and the glasses I see life through are from the mindsets that I have. Of course, any situation or circumstance that comes about will be seen through my lens of insecurity. This premise applies to any mindset that we have. I often say, "What you think about, you bring about!"

Sometimes it's hard to see our mindsets in action because we live in this world that we've created. It's like trying to look outside of a fishbowl when you're inside of it. It's really hard because every thought and feeling contradicts being on the outside when you're in the middle of it. My mindsets were definitely patterned throughout my life. Looking back now, I can see how certain ideals and perspectives that I had, good and bad, have shown up in every situation. One of the first memories that I could come up with after my daughter's passing was blaming myself for my failures. Regardless of the actual validity in that situation, it's a mindset, and so it carries itself into every thought in every situation, regardless of the fact.

It doesn't have to be true for it to be a mindset, even though we've convinced ourselves that it's true, because we feel that it's true. That's the tricky thing with our minds: with any idea we have, we can create emotions around it even though those emotions may not have anything to do with the current situation we brought them into. We've exported this emotional state from one situation to another. That's how powerful mindsets are. A healthy mindset will allow us to traverse difficult situations with ease because the mindset carries the emotional reality from one situation to the next. The same could be said for negative mindsets. I've realized that I blame myself for unrelated things; it's a mindset I can't shake sometimes.

Of course, I punish myself for it in different ways. I beat myself up mentally and emotionally until I'm exhausted enough to give in and forget about it until it comes back up. I fought this and have wrestled with it for a long time, but now I know it's a choice. And it took a lot of effort to reach this resolution. Most people accept that they have ideas, and those ideas produce emotions; they just call it their identity and say it is what it is. I am who I am, but if you blanketly accept every situation as your new identity, then we will be a construct of the worst situations in life. That will make us a permanent victim of the actions of others.

So the only way to see progress and change in our minds and our emotions is to have mindsets that can steer us into better places, quicker recovery, and more helpful ways of thinking. Not only will this enhance our lives because we're producing better emotions, but we are not creating an artificial world of the worst-case scenarios in our minds. Talk about torture. So many of us relive our negative experiences like a broken record every day in our minds. Sure, there's a moment in time that's helpful, but if lions are not chasing you, then a survival mindset is probably not the best one for you.

A great way to measure a healthy mindset is to ask yourself if the story you have today about certain relationships measures with the same passion, love, vigor, and thankfulness that it did once it began. As we look back, we're not reliving our past; we're asking ourselves what we perceive our past should be. It's a check-in with our minds, emotions, and hearts about the things we believe about the past. These check-ins happen in milliseconds daily, and we produce the feelings and thoughts that come with them. That's why the story we tell ourselves is so important, and our ability to reflect healthily is vital for our success today. Again, what we think about, we bring about!

I want everybody to be happy with me

Early on in life, I realized that it was hard to fit in, so I overcompensated and found ways to improve my relationships and get people to like me. I became a people pleaser. I couldn't handle the feelings and thoughts of being rejected, so I went out of my way to ensure I was liked. I hate this about myself. The temporary satisfaction of securing a relationship and having people like you is incredible. To meet someone for the first time and then have them want to be around you is a great feeling. But I couldn't shake the thought and the mindset of how the relationship started. Did they like me for who I was or what I did to make them like me? Of course, the imposter syndrome creeps in. I've got to keep acting like I did at the beginning of the relationship so they will continue to like me. Well, that gets exhausting because I'm always performing for everybody. Performances are tiring.

I can see how this mindset that I was carrying affected me. My self-esteem would diminish every time I dulled out a "sorry" for no reason. It was like the slow erosion of myself and my ego. I say this because I'm working on and aware of it. My mindset goes into everything I do. My relationships are affected by my mindset daily. When I look back in life, I only see through the mindset that I currently have. I can see how I've been a people pleaser in different seasons and what that has gotten me. This contributes to our struggle and tension. We can see how our mindsets have saved us and helped us through our past experiences, just as I brought up the survival mindset of running from a lion. It is a very helpful mindset to have in the right season at the right moment. But if I'm not in survival mode and I carry that mindset into my relationships into my future, then I will destroy everything around me, including myself.

I need to be able to see and distinguish how the mindset helped me in the past and where it let me down, and I need to be able to create a reflection that builds a new mindset for me today. Resiliency doesn't come from never changing; it's the opposite. Resiliency comes from constantly looking for ways for us to improve, adapt, refine, and persevere. However, to be truly effective at looking back at our past in a way that benefits us, we need to be open and transparent with ourselves about who we are. I've been very vulnerable with you in these past chapters; I've tried opening up my heart and mind so you could see what I was thinking, and feel what I was going through. There may be areas in my life where I still don't want to be honest with myself, and you will also experience that. Nevertheless, in the areas where I'm honest with myself, I can clearly see my mindsets and how they affect me.

My emotions

Emotions are amazing messengers. They communicate messages that are valuable and vital for our understanding and action. The interesting thing about emotions is that they're not always tied to our current reality. As I pointed out before, mindsets create emotions, and we can carry our mindsets from one situation to another. The same thing with emotions. This is helpful for us in developing consistency, understanding, and experience. I don't know if you've ever gone to a theme park, but generally, people have the same emotions when they think of theme parks. Well, how could your body give you an emotional response to the theme park experience that you haven't had yet? You can, because you had one before, or someone told you about it. You got really excited about theme parks when I mentioned that or you dread being in a line with a thousand people. You just produced an emotional response based on your previous knowledge or experience.

For illustration's sake, 50% of you just had a good emotional experience, while the other 50% had a negative emotional experience. What's the differential factor? It's how we reflect on our past. It's not what took place in our past; it's how we perceive our past because the same things happen at theme parks every day. You have crowded lines, overpriced food, people spilling their food items and wasting them, maybe your neck gets hurt on one of the roller coasters, and your feet hurt after walking too much. We have the same experiences, but our perception of what occurred is based on our mindsets. Some people think back to their theme park experience; it was heaven, and so much good came out of it. They can't wait to go back and do it all over again because they have gotten so much life from it. While others, you couldn't pay them to go to a theme park. The difference is what we make of it and how we perceive our past.

With a little healthy reflection, the people who think negatively about theme parks could be persuaded if their family told them how much it meant to them and how they got to spend time with their kids and grandkids. If a new restaurant opened, they would be excited about it because they love that kind of food. Maybe if they realized how much it made other people happy around them, then they would see more value in it. If they buy a theme park ticket and a dollar is donated to someone in need, they will go to more theme parks. These small considerations can change a mindset over time. It's like watching an elephant walk a thousand miles. One step at a time, and eventually, they'll get there.

What happens when our emotions are screaming at us, though? Or, worse, when we don't feel emotions because we've shut them down? For starters, we need to realize that our emotions are not the problem; they're simply trying to communicate with us. There are no bad emotions. I know we've all been taught in elementary school that there are bad emotions, but that's not true. We're taught everyone should exude all the positive emotions and shy away from all of the others. We're taught to perform for those around us so they only get the positive emotions, and we bottle up everything else.

This just means that our valid, strong emotions are being quarantined rather than understood and resolved. We bottle them up, and we hope and pray that no one can see that we're carrying them. Even though we act differently because we know that we've hidden them inside, this affects everything about us.

When I reflect on my past, the emotions that are produced are a great way for me to perceive it. What I think about Maddie and her life is how she's currently helping others with the organs she's donated and how her message affects the lives of thousands of people. I no longer have the feelings and the emotions of deep unresolved trauma as I once did when I heard the news of her getting hurt and being in the hospital. It wasn't simply the time between what occurred and now but my mindset about perceiving my past. Time by itself does not solve our emotional needs. We all know many people who have been stuck in the same emotional swirl for decades. Our mindsets are what change our emotional needs.

My biggest realization was that I could choose the emotions I experience when I think about my past. Some may consider this an override, but when I look back at Maddie's passing right now, I see all the good that came out of it, even the immeasurable good. The most healthy sense is that I am feeling good emotions through these new experiences, and it makes me want to help more people—to share Maddie's Message with everyone. But I know that was a choice I had to make long ago. Would I be someone who allows a negative experience to alter the course of my life, or would I use every experience that comes my way to my advantage, to my hope, to my future?

I don't necessarily feel like I've always had positive emotions about my past, but I haven't stopped pursuing what those negative emotions can bring me. One day, I'll look back on my past and have more positive emotions, but I also know that the strong negative emotions drive me and keep me going. We operate from a negative motivation cycle rather than a positive one. We go to work because we need money, and we know if we don't have money, then we'll starve so we're happy to go to work, and then there are those few select people who are a special breed who go to work because they love it.

Stop majoring on the minors

My son, Alex, used to ask for corn dogs for breakfast, and I told him no because that's ridiculous. Nobody's eating corn dogs for breakfast. But after Maddie died, I wondered why I care if he has a corn dog for breakfast. That's what he wants. He can have a corn dog. I realized that my priorities and the repercussions of my decisions had changed. In the course of life and death that I just experienced, it is inconsequential for my son to have one corn dog for breakfast, or even three. If it makes him happy every once in a while to have a corn dog, then he is having it. This moment, over breakfast, impacted me, and I coined this term as 'a corn dog experience'. I've often brought it up to my friends who have also experienced loss. If we're going shopping and my son wants to wear a Superman costume, I don't care. If it makes his heart happy, then let him do it. Life is too short and unpredictable. Eat the Corn Dog!

My incessant need to be a stickler or to hold control in every aspect of my kids' lives is no longer an option. Once you've lost a child, you realize the priorities that you have may be off. I'm more of a free-spirited, supporting mother now because I realized my sense of control and my perceived right way of doing things doesn't compare when it comes to loss. I get way more satisfaction now seeing my kids happy than I do controlling them. I learned not to major in the minors when I reflected on my past. These seemingly inconsequential things have no bearing on my true values of loving my kids and family and being the best mom. If you asked my kids if this is true, they may say I'm still controlling in some aspects, it's a journey for sure, but I know I've made tons of progress in this area. My older sons see it with Ellie, who is the baby in the family.

I went through a season of reordering and reflecting on the things I ultimately cared about and wanted to enforce. I realized that I stopped getting mad about the little things, and I had way more grace, understanding, and patience for the things that didn't matter. After you've lost a child, the comparison of what truly matters versus before is great. You stop getting frustrated at the little things because it's not worthy of your frustration anymore. This is one healthy way to reflect on our past. It helps us reframe the true values that we have today. What are your corn dog moments that you are ready to make happen? The time that you have with your loved ones right now is so precious. Be willing to allow them to have a corn dog when they want one.

Embracing healthy reflection

Learn to sit with your thoughts and not need to solve them right away. Our minds are constantly trying to offload their burdens and make quick decisions. When we're dealing with past trauma and loss, it's really healthy to just sit with one idea or thought and try to embrace it, look at it from all sides, and understand it. This will allow us to not so quickly dismiss these very important thoughts and emotions. The more we can embrace and understand the way we feel, the better we will communicate to others, and we will be more knowledgeable to get the help and change that we need.

Every reflection should come with balance. Our lives are not black and white, good or bad. There's a mixture in everything. This means we need to perceive our past in a more neutral light and decide what we want to do with that neutrality. Our lives are nuanced, and so is our past. Of course, losing someone is bad, but I'm also processing all the good that has come out of these situations. Do you see how we have to have a balance with the way we perceive and reflect on our past?

Healthy reflections must be a habit for us to create the change we want. This means we need to practice regularly. That's the only way habits are formed. Every time I think about a situation in my past that was traumatic, I need to go through a process with myself to make sure that it's a healthy reflection. They say most habits are formed in 90 days, so I would encourage you to, for the next 90 days, consider the thing that's the most troubling for you and set aside 10 minutes of reflections to properly position yourself to gain something from your past rather than feel 100% loss. What good came out of your past? What good could come out of tomorrow?

What I like to do, and what most people do in situations of trauma, is bury it and ignore it. It feels like the easiest thing to do because our trauma is so overwhelming. Unfortunately, ignoring it and burying it is not helpful. We need to think of trauma as a wound that needs to be taken care of. If there's an issue like trauma in our past, we need to address it, and we need to work on positive solutions that help us. If you're having trouble with this, make sure that you talk to people about your trauma, and talk to therapists, counselors, friends and family. It will bring you healing.

As we reflect on our past, we realize that it's really healthy to set goals to measure our progress. The goals don't have to be crazy. They can be small. For me, one of my goals was to get out of bed and do something good with the knowledge I have. Slowly but surely, those goals grew, and I was able to make progress into some really incredible things. I started from a place of trauma, and I was able to work myself out of it because of the goals that I set. If we set daily or monthly goals, we can set expectations to complete those goals. Many people who don't see progress in the area of trauma have not set any goals for themselves that are attainable and realistic.

One of the best ways for us to reflect on our past healthily is to practice gratitude. Gratitude is a secret enabler that takes information such as our trauma or past or our relationships, and it encourages us to look at our past in a positive light. The practice of gratitude changes our minds, slowly and surely. When we look back, our perspective on our past is reframed around the good, positive, and helpful things. Gratitude is one of the best ways to appreciate the little things and try to find treasure where there might be a mess. This reframing is healthy because it empowers us to live in the moment and not in regret. There are many resources on gratitude, and I would encourage you to look into it yourself if you think back on your past and trauma and you're not entirely grateful. One of the things I'm in a daily practice of is gratitude. Journaling what we are thankful for, and also putting something tangible in the hands of others to remind them that the world is still full of good people. I have designed a Random Act of Kindness card, which is a standard 4x6 notecard with Maddie's picture on it and our website for Maddie's Message. We leave this card behind when we do an act of kindness, like paying for the coffee for the person behind us at Starbucks or McDonalds, for example. It's also an amazing way to share the importance of furniture safety!

It's also okay to bring prayer into the darkest moments of our past. There's an exchange that happens when we pray to God. This allows us to reflect on our past through a Redemptive spiritual lens. It brings a context to a meeting that extends beyond ourselves. What would God have done in a situation? What does God think of this situation? What good could come out if God was involved? If we start to think about our past through the perspective of God, then we will find hope that transcends our thoughts and emotions, and promises a potential that exceeds anything we could have dreamed of. Prayer helps us do that, and as we pray, reflections about our past will change because our hearts are changing.

Looking back

When we look back now at our past, our loved ones, and even the situations that we've been through, how could we not see the most beautiful, hopeful thing? Number one, we can't change it, so what other options do we have but to accept it and find meaning and purpose from it? It has to be beautiful in some way. Every field of flowers is empty and barren at one point, but then, with the right ingredients and time, beautiful things can emerge.

How we perceive our past is nothing more than how we see ourselves today. Hopefully, after reading this book and others like it, you'll find some positive meaning and purpose in what took place. You'll notice over time that your perceptions will change based on your mood, mindset, and heart. It's easy to see this when we consider the relationships that we once had. They may have been the love of our life then, but now they're not so much. People that we didn't know at all are now everything to us.

We should be mindful of the thoughts that we allow in and realize that every thought and emotion builds something for us, and that building is what we live in. Are you happy with your own heart and mind, or are you at war with yourself over your past? I've often been the biggest accuser of myself over the years, and I fought myself hard for things I could control and couldn't. But as I've grown to accept myself for who I am, I've started to own my thoughts and emotions more, and rather than allowing them to lead me, I determine the path I want to go. My reflection is everything because it's the story I tell myself.

The story that I tell myself about what took place, who I am, and who I was should be one of hope, optimism, and love. The world gives us enough shame, resentment, and bitterness; why would we produce that ourselves? My story will be one of resilience, endurance, and commitment. I get to choose the story I tell myself, and my emotions, my mind, and my experiences will follow.

REINFORCE

We have to reinforce the good if we want to see sustainable fruit in our lives. This resilient structure needs to come from within, but we also need a supporting environment around us. We need to invite collaborative thoughts that build upon one another, collaborate, and help with our previous thoughts and emotions. In addition to that, we need to position ourselves to be around people and environments that support our growth. It's nearly impossible to do anything if we have toxic thinking about ourselves, or we're with people who are so pessimistic that they steal all the oxygen from the room.

The only way we'll see continued progress is if we ensure that the success we see in the healing, that we feel in the breakthroughs, that we experience is reinforced so that it doesn't become a one-off thing. We want to live our lives in a way that makes progress in our hearts and minds. We do this by reinforcing the good through sustainable, healthy mindsets and heart attitudes.

How do you know if you need to work on yourself more?

"They just don't make me happy anymore." It is an extraordinarily common phrase for those in relational conflict or who have given up. I fully understand if people are being mistreated. That's not being put into question here. The question here, however, is based on the level of happiness that you are expected to produce on your own. Of course, we want harmonious relationships where everything's reciprocal and we can expect and feel things from our partners, but who's in charge of your feelings? How can anybody possibly be in charge of your emotional state? If you sit down and think about it, the responsibility to produce the emotions you need is up to you. This is more of a cart before the horse scenario. Oftentimes, we export our emotional needs to the people around us because, maybe in an act of desperation, they are willing to jump in and help us when we're in an emotional struggle. This becomes a habit and a pattern where they jump in and do what they can to get our spirits up and make us feel better. This is extraordinarily common and about being kind and compassionate for those around us.

But at what point are we relying on others to continue to fill that void in us rather than building a sustainable reality for ourselves? This is when emotional intelligence comes in. It's the most proactive reinforcement tool for productive relationships with yourself and with others around you. The only way for me to have continued success with my emotions and my mental state is for me to have control. I don't have to rely on what others do and don't do for me to feel the way I need to feel. My happiness is not anyone else's job but my own. Of course, I want those around me to contribute to my happiness, but I can find health and wholeness outside their contributions.

This posture may take some getting used to for some people. Instead of showing up empty to the relationships and our past situations, we show up full. Instead of showing up to our partner needing a tremendous amount of positively reinforced input, we show up full. What does this do for both of us? Because of the heightened emotional awareness that each party is feeling and experiencing, they can address their needs promptly, respond to them, and communicate them more effectively. Instead of blaming the other partner for not fulfilling their needs because they should have anticipated them, everyone is empowered to manage their process. Therefore, our overall happiness should increase because we are responsible, empowered individuals.

Do you see the connection here with trauma and loss? I realized early on that nobody would come in and help me sort through my feelings and emotions unless I was willing to let them in. I realize that the way I feel is my responsibility to manage. I can't put that off on my children. I can't expect them, in their adolescent state, to accurately predict my emotional needs. I can't expect my spouse to accurately determine my emotional needs at any given moment. I need to reinforce my heart and mind so I can manage them myself and invite others to participate in my health, growth, and happiness.

The goal for us is to walk on our own two feet again. Sometimes, after trauma and loss, we need a lot of support and help. But we're not supposed to stay in bed or walk around the rest of our lives with emotional and mental crutches. We need to take the wins, the positive moments, and the progress, and we need to reinforce them so that they stay in place and we can succeed in our goals.

There's a clear distinction between people who see momentary relief because something or someone on the outside did something. It's like getting a gift from a friend. That may produce an emotion in you, which is a good thing because maybe it's your love language, but the question is, are you able to produce that emotion without that gift? If so, how often? Do you need external situations to provide momentary relief or an emotional experience? Can you distinguish the difference between the emotional experience you seek to have versus the ones you can produce on your own? Our continued emotional growth will reinforce positive behaviors and outcomes.

Focus on your strengths

Before encountering the traumas mentioned in this book, I knew enough about myself to be resilient and push through if given the opportunity. I guess, in a way, it was ingrained in me from early on. I have always felt that it is my responsibility to make things happen on my own in some beneficial way, which saved me during this crisis. I looked at myself in the mirror, and the only option was to push forward and work through any thought, feeling, or emotion I had. I may not have done it well, but I was moving forward. Of course, I was given the option to give up on myself because something so terrible happened to me. But what good will that do for myself and the people who need me? My family and the people I was working with depended on me. The only way I was going to make it through that trauma and have continued success down the road was to focus on my strengths, not on the things that I didn't understand, or my weaknesses. I doubled down on what I was good at.

Everybody has different strengths, and when you're creating momentum from trauma and loss, you need to grab hold of the things that you're good at, whether it's a mindset or an environment or a behavior, and as long as it's healthy and it creates growth and momentum, then you need to double down on that in this pivotal time. Focusing on reinforcing positive behaviors is about achieving a snowball effect, which is small wins that add to big things. If you're a really curious person, put your curiosity to work! If you are great at learning and self-educating, turn your living room into a library. If you are a really hard worker and can put your head down and work your way out of any emotional state, it's time to get to work.

It may sound simple, but why would we push aside the things that we are skilled at and something that we find pleasurable for something miserable? We do it because our mind is clouded and our hearts are confused. Something I struggled with, and I still do, is the feeling of loss and pain can also be present at the same time as joy and happiness, and even pleasure. I needed to be comfortable enough to be in the room with all those emotions simultaneously. Oftentimes, we shame ourselves for feeling good when we are in loss and pain. But healing comes with not only allowing those emotions to be in the same room as us—but as we introduce laughter, love, and joy, the other emotions rest in their proper spot.

In a moment of survival, our bodies get hyper-focused on the essentials, whether running, or swimming through frigid waters. Our bodies adapt and send all of their energy to the parts of our body for us to succeed. This is an incredible response from our physical bodies to help us make it through those moments; we do this emotionally as well. This is extremely beneficial but also detrimental if it's long-term. Our focus also needs to come with balance. We begin to acclimate as we graduate from these extreme emotional responses to something more balanced. The acclimation doesn't have the same stress response because we're used to our environment. We reinforce our healthy environment through acclimation. It's a question of whether we can acclimate to our emotional state or if we are jumping from zero to one hundred when we think of something. It's not a proposition to become numb but an invitation to regulate our minds and emotions. These actions make us stronger and more resilient and help us reinforce positive behaviors, producing better outcomes.

Remember your past successes

Something I introduced three years after Madison died was a celebration of her life. I made up some postcards—the Random Act of Kindness cards I mentioned earlier. We passed the cards out at this event in an effort to get our message out to the people outside of our inner circle. We attached 1,000 furniture straps to these cards and our Kindness Extravaganza began! Hopefully the person receiving it is inspired to do the same, but as a minimum, they're blessed with an act of kindness that they did not expect, and now they know about Maddie's Message.

This has been a delight to participate in. It's super fun when I get the chance to see the ripple effect of these Random Acts of Kindness. I found myself at the Verizon store one day and was talking to one of the employees about Maddie's Message. She was pregnant, which prompted the conversation and I gave her one of our RAK cards. Just then, the manager walked over. She came over wondering what we were doing. She looked down and saw the act of kindness card and realized they had just received one recently at a restaurant. As soon as she named the restaurant, I knew immediately that my friend, Erica, had paid for their dinner and had left this card. The manager was shocked and said I have that card on my fridge. We are changing lives one act of kindness at a time.

We mail these cards every year around Maddie's birthday and heaven dates. I also offer free furniture straps to be delivered to anybody who requests them from the nonprofit I set up in Maddie's honor. This repetitive participation in these acts of kindness cards reinforces a routine and a rhythm for me, my family, my nonprofit, and my community. It's healthy and helpful to look back every year and remember all the good we did. It reinforces more positive behavior moving forward. Your past successes don't need to be monumental. They can be small and incremental. Instead of lashing out at someone you love, you took a quick walk to cool your head. That's a tremendous achievement, and you should continue moving forward with that momentum. You may have had a really good day or month; that's a success. You should look at what you did differently to make it a really good day and month so you can repeat it.

Practice self-compassion

The world can be harsh, and the voice in our head can be severe. This is why we should practice self-compassion. When you're all alone with your thoughts and your mind is spinning, looking for the temperature in the room, the only thing you can pick up is negativity. You hear all the ways that you failed. Everything that you've done wrong. It's easy for our minds to pile up the negativity, and we beat ourselves up for it. Not only does this keep us isolated and stagnate, but it also hinders our growth and healing.

I'd be the first to say that sometimes the voice in my head is more regimented, and it gets me moving faster. When I'm harsh with myself, then I feel momentum, but I know the harsh critic that gets shit done isn't always the most helpful. This is where self-compassion comes in. If I can introduce self-compassion in between the moments of my momentum rather than criticism, then I can be kind to myself for all the effort that I'm putting in. I can be supportive of my actions that are making people's lives better because I'm willing to discuss my trauma and Maddie's Message. I realize the more I practice self-compassion, the more I will be able to give to someone else.

I get it; it doesn't feel productive sometimes because the critic gets so much more done. Rightfully so, I don't feel like I'm worthy of the kind, sweet words sometimes. Sometimes, I feel like shame and guilt are the only things that I should be getting. If I take 100% of the shame and guilt regularly, then where would that leave me? Believe me, I've tried, and it doesn't get me too far. I hate myself more for it, and I'm filled with resentment and sadness. In the same way that I chose not to be a victim, I also have to participate in a compassionate state that accelerates my journey.

The harsh, critical voice is a thief to our hopes and dreams. Eventually, the more we listen to it, the more we believe it, and the more we believe it, the more we act it out. That's why we should practice self-compassion and not always rely on harsh criticism to get things done or to keep us in our place. Even though we may feel the blame for what took place, and maybe we deserve that blame, self-compassion will help us make changes today so we can become the best version of ourselves and do the best through the pain we've experienced.

Helping others

The reward I often feel is not through a general sense of happiness, but from helping others. I can't possibly think about bringing myself to a place of happiness about the loss of my daughter, nephew, and brother—what I could do is make something good out of it. I can do this by utilizing the pain that I went through and the process of helping others through the same situations and experiences. When I feel the most rewarded, is when I help others. This phenomenon started after Maddie's passing. Of course, I helped my brother, family, and friends with the proceeding end-of-life care and funerals, but I also started helping others through various nonprofits.

When I received the phone call about Maddie's heart valves being donated to two kids in need, it was about four months after her passing. In the meantime, I was receiving support from LifeNet Health, the organ procurement company in my area. (Per their website, and through my experience, LifeNet Health is a global leader in regenerative medicine, organ and tissue donation, and life sciences. For nearly 40 years, it has been dedicated to saving lives, restoring health, and giving hope through innovative medical solutions. The organization specializes in tissue and organ transplantation, providing life-saving grafts and bio-implants for patients in need. It also plays a crucial role in scientific research, offering human cell-based solutions to advance medical discoveries. LifeNet Health operates worldwide, with a mission to honor donor gifts, improve patient care, and drive groundbreaking advancements in medicine.)

Other donor parents were able to speak about my process, and I was able to lean on them as much as I could and wanted to. After some time, I became a "Grief Companion" through their organization, and now I walk alongside others who are on their own grief journey. Providing the help these parents need. It's up to the parents to decide how much support they need. When I'm talking to these parents, I feel like I'm maximizing my knowledge and experience to help them through an extremely traumatic time. Maybe I'm giving them comfort, compassion, and direction so they can understand where they're at and make it through to the other side. I feel reinforced in my new role by giving back and supporting those around me in need. I know it was really helpful for me to receive that help, and now I can give it. Honestly, it's not even a question of whether or not I want to help someone who calls. I will move mountains to help them because it's the least I can do. Maybe the greatest thing that I could do.

Over time, I earned the credential as "the death expert." When someone dies, they call me and ask me what to do and what to say, and they lean on me for coaching and advice. This happens organically. I guess, in a good way, word got out that I've experienced severe trauma and I made it through. Perhaps they know that I've been through grief companioning and know that I help others with their grief. Maybe God sends them my way because he knows the healing it does for me to walk alongside others the way I wish I had had someone to walk alongside me.

I feel a sense of purpose in it, which reinforces all the good that I hope to envision with these situations. I dig deep down inside and try to give them the experience I had or didn't. If I feel alone trying to manage my own trauma, I try to give people on the phone a sense of connectedness and comfort so they never feel alone. I was harsh with myself and blamed myself a lot, so I try to reassure them that the more they lean on self-compassion, the better off they will be. Based on my personality type, I actually receive healing from helping other people. I may not have gone out of my way in a traditional sense to get help, but as I was walking other people through their pain, I was able to heal myself, and I've been helping others now for over 15 years.

Self-care & healthy habits

The best way to continue healthy habits is to reinforce them. A friend of mine and another PAT parent (Parents Against Tip-Overs), referred me to an emotional intelligence leadership training. She said you have so much untapped potential that you should do this training. She went through the training and got a lot out of it, so I agreed to do it as well. I intended to do this alone but was excited when my fiance, Ed, told me, "I don't want you to go and get emotionally intelligent and leave me behind, so I'm going with you." Ha! I love that we are on this journey together.

As we're going through the training, we're learning the same things, but we're all working through our own past process, and there's a lot of vulnerability required. Some of the training is online, and some parts of the training are in person and because of its intentionality, I've learned to be the most truthful and authentic version of myself. I wanted this help and needed this help for a long time, and it's this training that has been critical for my personal growth. There are a few things I've known in my heart for a long time, but could never find the words to articulate it. For example, I realize that I have never fully felt taken care of. To be clear, this is a me problem; I'm not blaming anyone for this. I've just gone through most of my life feeling like I had to take care of everything, including myself. Through this training, I realized this is probably why I have so many controlling tendencies. I didn't feel as safe as I could because of that.

This revelation came from this training, and I communicated it to my fiance, Ed. Not only did he embrace understanding me and realize that there were areas where he felt like he could contribute more and do a better job, but it also opened up our minds to the relationship that we actually have. If you were to ask me before this training, I would have told you that we had a nearly perfect relationship. Still, afterward, I realized all the ways I was overcompensating and correcting bad mindsets and behavior. I wasn't being honest with myself, I was not allowing anyone to help me, I needed this reset. Through the pursuit of understanding ourselves and self-mastery, we've improved our connection, communication, and love significantly. Now we have that nearly perfect, work-in-progress, extremely loving relationship I've always longed for.

We should all be a part of the constant pursuit of self-mastery. It's not that we need to achieve a perfect state where we're not able to make any mistakes, nor think freely. It's simply the journey to be a better person, spirit, soul, and body. I love listening to and reading anything from Mel Robbins, Amy Brown, and Bobby Bones. It's like they understand me and speak to different parts of myself in ways that others cannot. I try to surround myself with podcasts and new books that will challenge me to be a better person, and this ties into healthy habits that reinforce all the good that is taking place in my life.

The entire book is devoted to self-care and positive habits. I encourage you to incorporate self-care into your routine regularly. It may be something straightforward, like going for a walk every day for five minutes, or treating yourself once a week to something you feel refreshed from, like getting a massage or working out. Our self-care will change based on the season of life that we're in. My self-care this season is hanging out with my grandkids and reading a book. All these things will reinforce healthy habits so we don't get trapped spiraling backward.

Supportive environment & social connection

We can't do these journeys alone. You can't make it through hell and back alone. That's why we need supportive environments and reinforced social connections: when we're in need, we can rely on others to help us; and when they're in need, they can rely on us. An interconnected part of ourselves comes alive when we're in strong social connections. I realized early on in my process that if I connect with people who have been through similar trauma and loss, then I will feel a sense of connection and solace. I believe my purpose may come alive through this pain, and it has.

I propose to build strong connections with like-minded people, and therefore, I see the goal of making it through my grieving process much more efficiently. The common goal of solving furniture tip-over accidents became a focus. Together, we reinforced all the good we could to make purpose from our pain. We're there supporting each other, helping to bring clarity and understanding. When you're connected socially, you can feel a pulse and momentum. It's like feeling a heartbeat with its electric waves. If you're stuck, the group's momentum will push you forward. That's the difference between having a supportive environment and not having one.

I also find great outcomes through supporting each other and serving my family. I know there's a lot of science behind the reward center in our brain and how it responds when we go out of our way to serve others. That's when we receive a heightened state of happiness. Everything in my life is reinforced into all the good and what could come when I turn my heart and mind to help others. This is a choice that we have. We can participate and connect with others because it's the right thing to do, and we will be better off—or we can choose to be isolated and delay our progress. What are ways in which you can reinforce your dream, your hope, and your goals through your environment and social connections?

REIMAGINE

One of the greatest opportunities that we have in life is to create ourselves. There are moments in time when we're forced to recreate ourselves, and in my case, after my daughter died, I was given an opportunity. The opportunity allows me to use the most painful parts of my life for good. It gives me a purpose and a meaning that extends beyond normal work-life function and routine. To seize this opportunity, I need to look into myself and into my past and future and create a new world—one that can accommodate the new version of me, apply purpose and meaning to my pain and my trauma, and also help others along the way, because the greatest satisfaction we have in life is the efforts that we put forth for others.

In this chapter, we'll examine ways to properly position ourselves to reimagine what's possible as we decide to move forward in life. This may be an easy exercise for some of us, and it may happen naturally. Meanwhile, others are still dealing with the stages of grief and haven't reached these levels of acceptance. So, park this content in the appropriate spots of your journey.

By reimagining your life, you are saying you're worth it. You're saying that you're valuable enough to dream and think of ways to survive and thrive in the next season. We may never be the same after trauma and loss hit us. As a matter of fact, I know that I've personally changed. I've changed for the better. By reimagining ourselves and looking to not only apply context and meaning to our past and how we perceive it, but also looking at the depths of who we are and deciding who we are going to be, who we stand for, what we stand for, and what we are about. You're sensing a theme in this chapter from the preceding chapters because we're deciding not to be certain things or to be certain things. This internalized discussion is what we need to come up with.

By reimagining ourselves, we're not disowning or not valuing our past and what took place. I know my daughter died, as well as my nephew and my brother, and others around me. I'm not trying to write them out of my past and rewrite what took place. Still, rather, I'm trying to best utilize the best possible goodness that could come out of my life today, and that means I need to reassess who I am, how I look at myself, how I look at my past, and what I perceive to be available to me in the future.

I know this stuff is hard for some people because I've been to their houses. I've had conversations with them when something happened to one of their family members, and their bedroom is still the same. They haven't changed one bit. The car is still parked in the same spot in the driveway; the shirts are still hanging up in the closet. That is simply a manifestation of what's going on inside. The person's not ready to move on yet, they're not ready to reimagine themselves. They're not ready to create a world in their heart and in their mind where that person's not utilizing their things. And that's okay. It just means they're not ready to reimagine yet. The only good utility in keeping those possessions in their proper place, not touching anything, and allowing them to collect dust, is to keep the past the same. It means that we're not ready to adapt or change. We are not ready to take responsibility for the pain that we've endured. We have a glimmer of hope for those who are, and the idea of utilizing your pain for good is generally enough. For me, I saw no other way. I had already experienced pain in my life, and I wasn't going to sit around in this pain and not do something about it. So I put myself to work right away, trying to utilize everything I possibly could with this pain that I was experiencing so that it would do the best.

So curiosity got a hold of me, and I just kept researching. I started to apply myself to see what I could do and see, and what I could learn. There was a direct correlation between what took place, what I should be doing, and how I should be helping. For others, they may not have that same correlation, and that's totally fine. I know people who pick up exercise after they have experienced significant trauma, and the exercise allows them to reinvent themselves in a way. It's up to us, it's our life, it's our dream.

Reimagining our past

There are a few stages to reinventing ourselves and reimagining. One of the first stages is reimagining our past. If we're unable to do that, then we can't begin to reimagine things for ourselves, and we can't look to our future. Our past is the source of our greatest pain, and our perceptions about our past keep us in idle states of stagnation, or bring us the greatest delight and happiness. I needed to decide what I would think about my past and what wasn't allowing me the mental fortitude and resolve to create purpose and meaning for myself.

Looking back into our past, we often see the negative opportunities we missed. And the pain. We see these things because they help us survive, get to the next moment, and hopefully, not repeat our past. Well, that's a good thing. However, survival is not thriving in life, and survival is only essential for a few moments to get us out of a bad situation. We don't want to be in survival mode anymore. We want to be in thriving mode. How can I possibly recover from something like this? I don't know the answer for you specifically. But I do know this. If you learn to apply your pain to produce something good—whether for yourself, the people around you, or strangers—you will find more value and love than staying where you are. Again, we're not looking to rewrite our past and pretend it never happened, but rather look at our past and say how we can utilize the experience and the knowledge that we have, to do the most good.

One way I like to think of it is if I were to have a conversation with Maddie now and I asked her how I could honor her and love her the best with the situation being the same. What would she want me to do? The answer to that question pulls us out of selfish thinking and introspection, which sometimes doesn't help very much. When I hear the answer to that question, it feels like the best thing that I could possibly do. Also, asking that question frees me up from my initial emotional response. In a way, I'm fulfilling the mandate of happiness: working and serving others. Allowing the inner voice of Maddie to help me decide how I can best serve her in honor of her opens me up to joy and love that I wouldn't have received otherwise. I know that may sound weird, but at the end of the day, it's just emotional intelligence. I think about and perceive what the other person wants and needs, creating an opportunity to make it happen.

Our pasts are confusing and complex. If we have unresolved emotions, they cloud our judgment about our past. So rather than trying to bring about every answer and address every need, let's tackle it from a different perspective, rather than looking at our past and demanding to know the truth and demand answers from God. Let's tackle our next steps by changing course. Let's suspend our ultimate desire to have all the answers before we're able to move forward. When we jump into a car to drive it, we don't understand how all the parts and components work inside the car, but we trust that it should work. We're willing to give it a try. We don't need to know everything about what happened, what didn't happen, and what should have happened so we can look at our past differently. I'm not saying that you shouldn't seek answers or wisdom; they can be helpful. I'm saying don't allow the lack of knowledge to cripple you from moving forward, because you're worth it.

So, what does reimagining our past mean? Our past, or the recollection of our past, is the current version or narrative of what we believe happened. Because we're unable to relive our past, we have a version of events in our emotional and cognitive processes. We look at our past and start to reimagine it in a different light, one that is not overly bearing on the trauma and the loss and the pain, but rather on what good could come out of our past. Our perception of what happened and what we're doing about it changes. Healthily, we start to look at our past and see a redemptive value that applies purpose and meaning, not just loss. My faith allowed me to see good in something that would be a parent's worst nightmare. Of course, I feel sadness, and my heart breaks all the time, but now I have an outlet for my pain that is useful.

For me, the direct outlet was thinking about ways to share my time, wisdom, expertise, and experience with others who had the same needs. I decided to help others, especially newly bereaved parents, and walk them through the same process that I went through. I decided to get into prevention, which involves supplying furniture straps for the practical needs of others, so they can prevent these disasters from happening to their families. I decided to write a book because I saw the value in teaching others about Maddie's Message and the story of resilience. It's not a perfect story. I'd be the first to say that I don't have it all together, and sometimes, I question whether I have anything valuable to say. I'm applying myself to do the best with what I have.

So I looked at my past, and I continue to look at my past, and I don't just see trauma, and I don't just see the loss. Still, I see the love, and I see the help, and I see the two little lives that Maddie's heart valves were affected by, and I see the thousands of acts of kindness cards that we've sent out every year, and I see the parents that I've been helping this month and last. When I look at my past now, I see that it motivates me to help others, it motivates me to create, and to move. Looking at my little daughter's face brings purpose and meaning to my life because I'm allowing her story to be heard, felt, and experienced. What are ways in which you can reimagine your past in a more redemptive light?

What's the plan?

To create a new skill set and habit, we need to put together a plan of action. This might require us to develop new skills and stretch ourselves in ways we couldn't have imagined. As we move forward in this new endeavor and season, we need to see through the lens of optimism and hope. Granted, everything we hope for and desire is impossible, but we can find hope in possible things. We might feel inferior, unable to put a dent in such a significant issue that's presenting itself before us, but you don't know what's possible because you haven't tried it yet.

We need to be able to work from what we know rather than what we don't know. This means we must put on our critical-thinking hats and develop solutions that weren't available. For starters, you just have to identify the problems, brainstorm solutions, and implement a resolution effectively, which can empower you to overcome the challenges you may face. As we change the way we think to become more solution-oriented, it will renegotiate our efforts, and our energy will be spent much more effectively on proactive things.

This comes with a growth mindset. There's much to say about growth mindsets, but we need to think in a way that allows us to expand our horizons. It allows us to build and move forward. Our thoughts should motivate us to change and achieve our goals and objectives. If we don't have goals, we need to set them because the easiest way to find disappointment is to not set any goals and have no achievable outcomes. At one point in my life, I needed help getting out of bed, and I'm so grateful for it. This may be your time to get up and apply yourself. Don't let excuses hold you back. You're worth it. The pain and trauma that you've endured are worth it for me—Maddie's worth it.

One of my favorite parts about planning is having the ability to dream. Dreaming is a fun and important stage. Not everybody can facilitate opening up a realm to dream about what's possible. But we need to be able to enter a dream stage every now and then to help us see something outside our current season, and beyond our current realm of influence and possibility. We need people who can think creatively and dream up solutions and possibilities that weren't available before. This may include new inventions with a functional use that could prevent accidents, change laws, and make a difference in life.

When we dream, we can think of things that propel us forward. They may not make sense at the time, but our dreams often do. Most things we enjoy in tremendous ways today come from a dream, like flying in a plane and riding a bicycle. All of those things came from moments of dreaming. I know dreaming may be difficult for some because we're using our pain to motivate us into these dreams, but isn't it the best use of our pain, rather than letting it be unmet and unresolved?

It's the opposition principle that motivates us sometimes. The thing that we feel is the most resistant is what we need to press into, because it's our invitation. For me, my pain in losing Maddie has motivated me and propelled me to act in ways that I could not have imagined, and the Lord knows what the results of my charitable work have been. I do believe, though, that as people grasp hold of this message and turn their pain into something useful, inventions will emerge, lives will be saved, and movements will be started to improve our planet, prolong life, and bring more enjoyable moments into our day. If someone has been through trauma and loss and becomes resilient, they are unstoppable, and that person is you.

Reimagining my future

I knew I had to change the minute that she died. Not only did I want to become a better person for my family, but I also knew I had to change personally. Carri 2.0 came out. The old version of me was no longer, and the new version emerged. I did a complete makeover. I reassessed how I thought about things, how I considered life, how I led my teams at work, and how I managed my free time. Looking at my past differently allowed me to restructure my day in the present moment.

I wanted to share Maddie's Message and deliver furniture straps to people. The first thing I did was set up a website. I just wanted to share our story on the website, educate people. This is not about selling anything or making money; it's solely about education. I just wanted her message to get out so people could understand the risks of not having your furniture strapped to the wall. I wanted to tell people that the furniture in your house is dangerous. Anchoring furniture is not only cheap, it's easy. I wanted to put a face to the tragedy. Seeing her sweet little face and her cute little piggy tails made it more real. Seeing her face prompted more people to act on the information they knew.

After a few years of having the website up, I turned it into a nonprofit. I kept asking myself what I would do to honor her legacy and message. Eventually, I came up with Maddie's Message and a nonprofit organization that buys furniture straps in bulk and gives them away. This not only allowed a mechanism for her message to get out, but it also established a bunch of credibility.

It allowed me to advocate on her behalf on Capitol Hill in Washington, DC, along with eight other parents who lost kids in the same way that I lost Madison. Not only did I share Maddie's story with anyone who would listen, but I also advocated on her behalf to the U.S. Consumer Product Safety Commission, a federal government agency that works to keep Americans safe by protecting them from unreasonable risks of injury and deaths related to consumer products.

We call ourselves PAT (Parents Against Tip-Overs). After finding out the stats the week that Madison died, I was thinking about the kids who were losing their lives and getting injured every single month. It's estimated that 20,000 kids a year hit the emergency room due to furniture tip-over accidents; that's one kid every 17 minutes, and every 11 days, a child dies from the same accident.

In 2019, I became actively involved in PAT, a national nonprofit organization dedicated to raising awareness and preventing furniture and television tip-over incidents. Our mission is to support, educate, and drive change to protect children and families from these preventable tragedies. Since its inception, PAT has advocated for tip-over prevention through education and regulatory efforts. We provide anchoring resources, public service announcements, and educational materials to help families secure the furniture in their homes. PAT parents were key stakeholders in creating and advocating for the Stop Tip-overs of Unstable, Risky Dressers on Youth (STURDY) Act, a piece of national legislation that requires stability be built into clothing storage units that are sold in the United States. The bill was signed into law in December 2022, and it gave manufacturers until September 2023 to comply.

This is huge because manufacturers, including large ones like Ikea, are now required to meet this new safety standard and help save lives. We had sponsorship from several U.S. Senators, including Senator Casey in Pennsylvania, and worked closely with Ikea and several other key stakeholders to advocate for its passage. It was a bittersweet process because we discovered a lot of negligence, but we could also implement this law, which would help prevent so many tip-overs. The whole STURDY process took five years to pass and another year to implement.

Hopefully, with these changes, we can make more progress and prevent our children from becoming statistics. This bill doesn't work for old furniture or secondhand furniture, so furniture straps are still very necessary. If you own furniture that is manufactured prior to September 2023, it may not meet the new minimum safety standards and may be more susceptible to tip-overs.

Through Maddie's Message, we are able to put on local events—including speaking events, 5K runs, and others—to build awareness. Most of the time, I find myself in the grocery store line, convincing the person in front of me that they need to strap their furniture to their wall. Whenever I see someone with a young child, I hand them a card and give them some furniture straps. Of course, if you want to buy them alone, they're about $1.25 apiece.

In addition to my work through the nonprofit, I spent some time working with LifeNet Health. Not only did they help me, but I was able to give back by helping them as a grief companion for newly bereaved parents. They just so happen to be located in the same city I live in, so I connected with their leadership and came in and did training for their call center. Imagine having a job at a call center that connects with people who've lost loved ones and are trying to procure their organs for donation. What an incredible group of people and an incredible set of circumstances. I shared with them ways I was helped and how they could handle their customers to understand things from a parent's standpoint. They have been incredible, and I have nothing but positive things to say about them. My daughter's organs saved two lives. I would encourage everyone to become an organ donor. (www.donatelife.net)

A few thoughts that I processed with them are included in this chapter. As I reimagined my current situation for the future, one thing that has always been top of mind for me was what it really meant to say yes to organ donation. When you think about it, two families had been praying for heart valves for their children. Who knows how long they have been waiting. Their prayers were answered when Madison died, but it's more than that. In order for their prayers to be answered, a HEALTHY child had to die. They needed HEALTHY organs. The only way for that to happen is through a tragic accident. A healthy child that dies tragically in a car accident, a drowning, or even a furniture tip-over. It's a profound way to reimagine how this all worked together for good. God has reminded me many times over, *"And we know that all things work together for good to them that love God." Romans 8:28 KJV*

I believe people have been placed in my path by design. Shortly after my daughter died, I had a lady on my team whose child died in the bathtub. I would never have known what to do, how to do it, or what to say before. Because I had just experienced my own child dying, I was able to walk beside her on her journey and help her along the way. She leaned on me for the next steps, thoughts, considerations, and direction. I realize it's my job to help these people because they have similar needs, and I have a unique experience that could benefit them now. That's how I reimagined my life.

I recently spoke at a conference to about 400 women. The topic, you guessed it. "Don't wish you would have." The amount of people that came up to me afterwards and shared the topics that they could relate to, was incredible. Whether it was the loss of a child, or close family member, or even something I had shared about my own career path. I was able to encourage them to apply themselves, find resilience, and see a path forward that will enable them to utilize their story to bring about the most good. That's how I reimagined my life.

It takes time and space to reimagine. It's not something we can typically do right away. Sometimes, life helps us sort out our past and perceptions of ourselves. We need to be in a stable place before we can reimagine who we are and who we want to be. We should think of our lives as the most significant opportunity we've been given, and we should take the cards dealt to us and use them to the best of our ability. It doesn't need to be monumental. It can be simple. You can choose to turn your pain and loss into kindness and be kind to everyone around you, become the best employee your company has ever had, or become the best parent, grandparent, brother, or sister. You decide how you want to reimagine yourself and how you could apply yourself. The opportunity is yours because, in this precious life, there's nothing greater than fulfilling the desires of our heart.

RESOLVE

I always wanted to look back and be proud of how I handled my moments of loss and pain, how I responded to them, and all of my future actions. It's been messy at times, and I know that I've had to push through both personal and situational obstacles that would prevent me from achieving optimal success.

The tension comes with trying to create a new process, new emotions, and a new life. Dreams don't happen overnight, and goals don't make themselves come to pass. There's a persistence and a process that should be used for everything we want. Instead of being a passive receiver of life, I prefer to direct and orchestrate the monumental moments of my life as much as possible. It doesn't always happen the way that we hope it will, but the more we plan and the more we're able to execute on our terms, the greater our level of satisfaction will be.

What do we do when stagnation and depression are not an option? We have to get creative. We have to develop goals, even small ones, for ourselves. It could be getting out of the house and meeting somebody new today to break out of that shell we've built for ourselves. I know it's not always going to be easy. We don't set goals because they're going to be easy. We set goals because they're meaningful and purposeful and give our life significance. If we were looking for an easy route, we would be looking for something that doesn't exist.

We choose what kind of arduous journey we want—if you isolate yourself, it's difficult when no one's there to take care of you and when no one's there to support you. When you're in a relationship, some difficulties come with that. You may get into an argument, have conflicts, and feel lost. Is there an easy path in life? I don't think there is. So, what are we left with? Apart from wallowing in our misery and declaring defeat, we could address the most significant opportunity in front of us: to make something beautiful out of what we've been given. This means we must set some goals and show up meaningfully to make them happen. If you don't want to do it for yourself, you surely have someone else in mind for whom you would set a goal. It takes courage to set goals and create expectations; but sometimes, expectation is the furthest thing from what we want to do. Expectation means we must show up and rely on others, and that's not always fun.

Sometimes, it's so much easier to keep our thoughts to ourselves and not place any perceived burdens on ourselves because we expected something to happen and it didn't happen the way we wanted it to. Isn't that just fear labeled as something else? We may have these fears holding us back from doing something great, worthwhile, and doing something with tremendous life and meaning. It may be as simple as loving the person next to us. Everyone has their context for meaning and purpose. But after you've taken some time and considered how to rebound your life, reinforce all the good, and reimagine what was possible, it's time to make it happen.

Some of the characteristics we need to succeed may not be natural. We might not find ourselves with grit, determination, poise, and focus. I mean, we've been through trauma, and that's not something that comes easy for people who have been through it, right? But what if we redirect our pain into something meaningful on a continual basis until we see lasting change within ourselves and the world around us? We're all driven by different things, so rightly placing our drive toward something beneficial will bring us health, and create a meaningful purpose for us to pursue.

I've always wondered if our pursuit in life is a monumental thing or something that's passive. The more I consider it, the more our individual small micro-decisions become a composite of our overall pursuits in life. When we're sitting alone in our thoughts, thinking about ourselves, our past, and our future, those little moments define our pursuits more than any grandiose display. It's like when you get married; you've already decided to marry the person before you step out and say 'I do'. If you were not to think about it until you get to the altar, then you would probably be in for a surprise, and not be a good one. Seems so silly, but it's true.

Because we shape our pursuits every day, we need to have a steadfast resolve in who we are, what we're about, and our goals. Based on that, I believe that if I didn't have something to pursue, then my situation would overtake me. I know enough about myself that if I stay put and don't do anything, I just become a miserable mess. I've got to act because movement is life. I might not get it right all the time. I plan on making mistakes, but I will be determined to keep moving forward.

It's easy for me now to show up and be excited about Maddie's Message and what it could do to help millions of lives. My efforts make an impact! The effort that I have put forth over the last 17 years helped me do something that's monumental to completely change the way that kids are affected by these preventable causes. I can help change the statistics across the board and completely revolutionize parenting to save kids from preventable causes. My efforts today may pave the way for my success tomorrow. How will I know if I'm not determined to find out?

What are your goals?

After making it halfway through this book, you can consider some small micro-goals for yourself. You might not consider them goals, but consider them in the following steps. I know some of you may want to be happy again, and you place so much expectation and satisfaction in what you had that you've convinced yourself it's impossible to be happy again. So, finding happiness is a goal of yours. It may not be in the same thing or person that you once enjoyed happiness from, but it may be in something else. In my case, I currently derive a lot of satisfaction and happiness when I'm helping others in their moment of need. That kind of happiness differs greatly from the happiness I received when Maddie was alive. They're not replaceable, but it's a goal that I have to continue to be open to alternative ways to bring about my happiness.

Some of you may be considering a way to love, find a significant other, or trust again. Rather than listening to all the excuses and reasons why you should stay isolated for the rest of your life, and die on a hill somewhere alone, have you considered all of the good that could come out of opening your heart up again? The question I asked people who had former relationships and are looking to love again right now is, what did you get out of that past relationship? Whether it was love, connection, satisfaction, friendship, or whatever it may have been, do you think it's impossible to find those same connections and pleasures in another person? Of course, it's not. We don't want to try. So, how do we take baby steps toward loving again? I would say one of the first things to do is to get some friends and put yourself in situations where you get to meet new people. See, those baby steps weren't so daunting or catastrophic.

Whatever your goal may be, you're working towards it. The journey may be impossible, like the one that I've taken. I desire to stop all furniture tip-over accidents in America. That could be an impossible goal, but I needed a goal bigger than myself for me to be fully involved. And I know it brings tremendous meaning to all of those who have had preventable deaths. Sometimes, we need something bigger than ourselves to show up and participate. I know people, including myself, who consider what God would think and say regarding our actions. I'm driven by a sense of morality and spiritual influence because I know our lives have intrinsic meaning to God.

Whether your goals are big or small, they should be something you're working on and applying yourself towards. I know it's been over 17 years since I lost Maddie, and time feels like it's just flown by. Because it has. I could have just let those 17 years go by without doing anything about the preventable loss that I experienced. Instead, shortly after we buried her, I jumped in and applied myself to make something out of this mess, and I'm so glad that I did. I know I may not work on Maddie's Message every day, but every day it's on my mind. Still, the momentum I've created with so many others to bring awareness to furniture safety and change legislation, as well as prompted many acts of kindness, has created a movement. I live for that; it brings me purpose and sends a clear and resounding message to my pain, indicating that it was all worth it.

How many reasons do you have to push through the pain?

Goals just don't happen by themselves. The very reason that they are achievable is because they're hard. It wouldn't be a goal unless it had a measurable resistance level. When a baby starts taking their first steps, putting a goal in place is easy because they haven't taken steps before. But after walking for 30 years, you don't wake up in the morning and say

I have a goal to walk today, because there isn't any present resistance to that idea. Now, the goals that we have after trauma and loss might seem inconsequential to those who haven't experienced what we have, but to us, they are monumental. And for that, we need to find the fortitude and grit to push past unbelievable emotions, doubts, and personal failures.

We're trying to accomplish something that might be the hardest thing we've ever done, with the greatest resistance given what we've had to overcome. How does one accomplish things that don't make sense to the logical mind? When we have a clear reason for what we're doing before, we are willing to traverse mountains and complete impossible missions. I know I've been a hard worker, but I've never once thought about passing legislation and working on preventable deaths. It never once crossed my mind. But it felt easy to accomplish because I had a clear reason for who I was doing it for. I'm not saying it was easy, but in comparison to who I was doing it for, everything felt easy. I was happy to do it and the work was put in the framework of my passion and desire to do this for Maddie.

When you look within yourself and can't find the reasons to do something, it's best to look outside yourself for inspiration. When our emotions are pressing in on us, and we're exhausted because we're overworked and overloaded, we may have to dig deep into places we've never been inside our hearts and minds to make the small steps possible. That is, fortitude and grit. Maybe you've been told that it can't be done and will waste your time. Now, you have an opportunity to prove somebody wrong and the motivation to do it.

We may need to prove something to ourselves by accomplishing these goals. I guess whatever motivates you is a good thing. Eventually, though, the realization of the promise should take over. What are you fighting for? What are you living for? Who are you living for? Whether it's legacy, inheritance, parenting, unconditional love, or the promise of what could be, we all have a reason to deliver the best version of ourselves and show up and crush all of our goals.

We are going to see challenges and obstacles.

It is all but certain that we're going to see challenges and obstacles with every goal that we face. Still, those moments where we push through the obstacle and show unwavering determination and firmness of purpose allow us to manifest our desired outcome. The journey through resistance is what forms us. Sometimes, it's the goal, like fighting to end world hunger. Perhaps we're able to make significant changes with that particular goal, but the journey itself is what forms and shapes us.

The number one obstacle we will have as we pursue these promises and goals will be with our former selves. We will find a way to convince ourselves that we're not worthy, or we're too busy. Who are we to try to accomplish something like this? We can devise a million reasons why we shouldn't pursue this goal or this promise. Maybe we are the reason for our trauma, and we just need to get out of the way, rather than cause more harm. Right? Wrong. We need to overcome these obstacles and fight through our perceived failures.

The obstacles in front of us are an opportunity rather than a reason to quit. If someone's looking for a reason to quit, they will always find it. We can't look at our goals and excuses and justify a way out. Whenever we get into doubtful swirls, we should just remind ourselves why we are doing what we are doing. And remind ourselves of why it's worth it, why we are worth it. Why is it worth it to accomplish things for others? Rather than looking at our small measurable goals as an end-all to our mission, we need to see this as a lifestyle and a journey. If we can somehow make this a part of our lives, we will see the obstacles and the problems as a part of the process and not be surprised by them. They become characters in the drama. We expect them to perform at certain points during the story. See, it's a matter of expectation; if we expect certain problems to come up, they won't derail us or throw us off guard because we know they're coming.

We will be our number one obstacle, so we must use tenacity and persistence to stay strong and refuse to give up early and easily. This decisiveness will help us push through the moments when we don't feel like doing anything. We don't feel like making progress today. When all the excuses come in, we are able to push through and work diligently toward the goals in mind, and you'll be surprised that you'll begin to find your purpose in the mission rather than in your feelings. Your feelings will become secondary to what you're accomplishing. If we can find the fortitude and grit within ourselves, then what we desire to do will become easy and accomplishable. It might still be bigger than ourselves but show up every day and do our part. Once we're committed to achieving an outcome, deep-seated commitment can help us accomplish those objectives.

But you're going to have to be brave

One of the hardest things I've ever done is face my fears and failures. It's not even something I feel like I have fully conquered. But in some redemptive way, my small baby steps to facing those fears and failures have accomplished great things. I've helped change people's lives because of my ability to overcome a little bit of my struggle. I know what it feels like to have your heart ripped out of your chest because of the tremendous loss you've experienced. I know what it's like to wake up in the morning and ask yourself the reasons why you still want to live. I know what it's like to feel numb. I know what it's like to wake up in the morning, look at yourself in the mirror and not like what you see. But deciding to show up and participate to love, give your best, and do it anyway proves all of our fears wrong.

Whenever I'm having difficulty building up the courage to show up that day, I look at Maddie's cute little face on this postcard I made. Somehow, her face still gives me the courage to talk to people I don't know, encourage them to make changes in their home even though I've never been there, and interrupt their day. Boy, do I feel the inconvenience of saying excuse me, do you know about furniture tip-overs? I know they're not planning on talking to me; it's tremendous and inconvenient for some people, and some days, I don't want to do it. I'm just not feeling it. But when I reach inside my purse and pull out one of those postcards, I remember why I'm doing what I'm doing, why it's all worth it, and why I must be brave.

Finding the good

It's impossible to be discouraged if we always find the good in what we do. We could have a thousand obstacles and a thousand things going wrong, but if we can find one good thing in our efforts, it will be worth it. Resolve is often categorized by tireless perseverance and refusal to be discouraged. We can forge ahead and do impossible things if we can keep our minds right and look ahead to all the wonderful things we're doing.

This doesn't always need to be an astronomical thing. Finding the good could be the smallest amount of good possible and determining that it was worth it. It's like talking to someone and sharing a message with him. Maybe they will fully reject you, which has happened to me many times. Instead of finding a reason to give up and convincing ourselves that nobody wants to talk to us and nobody cares, perhaps we raise ourselves and determine that they will probably think about what I said when they go home. You know what? It might cause them to act on my advice. So now, it is justifiably worth it, even though they rejected me.

Sometimes, persistence helps us overcome ratios and odds that are against us. We know that not everyone in the world wants to hear what we have to say or wants to adopt something we have in mind. We know that rationally, but when we encounter people in the real world, we get offended because some people say no. If we built an expectation that not every person would accept us right away, we wouldn't be so distraught when we hear a no or get rejected.

One percent change is all that we're looking for. When we try to climb a mountain, the mountain is obviously larger than life; if one were to try to climb it in a few steps, it would be impossible. So why do so many expect themselves to accomplish mountain-top experiences with only a few minimal efforts? The only way to climb mountains is to do it one step at a time. This is the 1% rule. It's measurable, achievable, and it's not overwhelming.

If we perceive our progress and our change with the 1% rule, then we can muster up the strength, courage, and bravery to make a 1% change. That seems doable, and slowly and surely, over time, we will accomplish our entire goal. One step at a time allows us to see the progress that we're making.

Hold on to those wins and good days. Our minds love to cling to negativity and convince us otherwise. If we can hold on to those good days and wins, then we'll constantly be reminded of when it worked out, when we saw a breakthrough, and when we helped someone. We need to hang on to the good moments because sometimes they don't happen every day, and the testimony of when it worked should remind us of all the good that we've done and who we've helped. I am a superfan of Bobby Bones, of the iHeart morning radio show, The Bobby Bones Show. He has a bit every hour on his show called "Tell me something good." I have listened to him for years and have incorporated this bit into my daily life. During my staff meetings, we go around and everyone "tells us something good." It's the positivity, the purposeful action of looking for the good in life that changes your mindset.

The endurance of life

It's so easy to compartmentalize our lives and forget that we're on a journey. We wake up in the morning and go to work; we plan our evenings with our family, and our weekends are full of errands. It's easy to let time run away from us, and some of us can look back on the last couple of decades and wonder what we accomplished apart from binge-watching the new Netflix series that comes out every week. If we can find a way to weave our goals and our promises to ourselves into the fabric of our day, then we will develop an endurance for life.

When our hearts are in the right spot, we can turn the mundane into the magnificent, but it will take a lot of self-determination and commitment. For me, Maddie's Message is nothing more than the slight inclusions I incorporate into my day, regularly. I don't go out of my way to make these moments happen anymore. I bring Maddie's Message with me wherever I am. It's a part of my normal life now, and I don't consider it a burden—it's a lifestyle.

Looking back now, we can surprise ourselves with the things that we've overcome. The struggle seems overwhelming and impossible because it's nothing we could have ever imagined. As we can now separate ourselves from our past through time, we can look back and realize that we made it through by the grace of God, the help of others, and every ounce of courage we had. We made it through, and we're still standing. Curious minds want to know why. Why didn't it crush us completely and ruin us? Is it because we were helped? Is it because we have a message and a movement to participate in? It could be because of the promises in our lives. It could be because the people around us need us. Whatever the reason may be, it saved us so we could do something great with our lives.

Our lives will only have intrinsic meaning and purpose if we apply ourselves to what we know and have experienced. We can't quit. We can't back down. We can't give up on ourselves because some people need us. They are the reason why we want to become a better person. Why do we want to show up more, love better, and bring excellence? We may not like running the race daily, but we're making progress. Once we find the resolve necessary to overcome the current obstacles, we can march forward into the promises available. If you ever get off track, remember why you're doing what you're doing. Whenever I am a little confused, tired, or flustered, I remember her face, and I get the clarity and motivation that I need because she makes it all worth it.

CHAPTER 10

TELL YOUR STORY

Perhaps one of the hardest things that we may do after we experience trauma and loss is finding a way to talk about it. We have our self-perceptions and relationships, where we all try to manage each person's expectations. We want to share the details of our lives, but we don't want them to impact our relationships negatively. Maybe they'll think about us differently if they only knew what happened. Can you relate? So we're willing to endure an internal struggle of trying to quarantine parts of our lives away from other people. This only produces a diluted form of self, and an exhausted one. Not only do we have to keep up with multiple images of ourselves and find out what story we told this person versus what story we told that person, while we're maintaining these spinning narratives. It's exhausting. We feel a tremendous protection over our individual stories because we're trying to maintain an image so people will like us. We don't know exactly how they will respond when we tell them the truth.

It's scary, and I had to confront it right away on my journey. My loss was very real, and it's not something I could have just discounted at work. I was even trying to manage it myself, and it wasn't working because my trauma was spilling out onto all the other employees. For starters, handling these events is not something we should do alone. We should find courage within our journey to be able to talk to other people about it. As I mentioned before, one of the most helpful things for me was to find a group of people who had been through a similar experience, so we could work together and process together. Putting myself in that environment diffuses my inclination to want to isolate. This puts me in front of others, and when I'm with people, I'm excited to share my story, my journey, and Maddie's Message.

Not everyone is wired the same, so the idea of connecting with people on the phone about their past trauma or speaking in front of large groups of people can be daunting for some. The goal of opening up is not so that we can all become public speakers. The goal is to become free and not be bound by these artificial reservations. So we can own our story and our journey and not let our internal hesitations keep us from moving forward and advancing in life. This is going to look different for everybody. For some people, it will be a process of developing enough courage where you're willing to tell a therapist, counselor, or a friend. We all have different goals in mind, and the ultimate goal is for us to be able to feel liberated and not restrained by our process. It doesn't mean that we have to tell everyone. Of course, we have boundaries in mind, and as I've pointed out before, some people just don't treat us the same, so why would we give them something of value if they're going to dismiss it?

We want to find a healthy balance for our goals, but also realize that the healing nature of talking about our story is practically essential. If we were to share openly about our goals and discuss our trauma, for the majority of us, it's not going to be at the top of the list. That sounds more like a burden than something that would be great. I mean, who wants to discuss their mistakes, failures, and worst pain points? Not very many do. Not many do because they have not yet reached the level of healing to see the value in sharing their story.

Reasons to share

We want to open up and share our story for two primary reasons. First and foremost, we do it for ourselves. We do it to free ourselves, find healing, find connection, find commonality, and bring ourselves back into the normality of life. That is an incredible part of finding an outlet to help us move forward and achieve our new goals. The second reason we open up and share our story is for others. It could be how we experienced healing in the first place; we listen to others to help us along our journey.

When we share, we impart wisdom, encouragement, love, understanding, and create a path of communication and connection with those around us. That interconnectedness brings us tremendously closer to our goals than if we were to try to do it alone. One of the first things we often realize when we open up is that we're not alone. It may seem simple, but if we were to go around life not sharing, we would feel like no one gets us, understands us, or can relate. If we just share our process with others, we'll realize that we're not alone and other people are experiencing similar things. It may seem simple, but we do it all the time.

And what's the point of overcoming some of the greatest obstacles and challenges thrown at us, and not talking about them with anyone? Our story is one of our most valuable things, and the only person who can take that away from us is ourselves. We're the only ones who can restrict our speech and process.

There's a really cool thing that happens when we open up to those who are around us. We cannot only impart wisdom and experience and perspective about our growth journeys, pitfalls, and pain points, but we can also unlock them into new avenues that they might not have considered before. Let's talk about what has been holding them back their entire lives. It's not uncommon that people come up to me after I'm done sharing—they find an element of my story that they can relate to, and it gives them courage and strength to pursue their goals and become better people. Sometimes I'm the first person they've ever shared with. It's liberating, It's also humbling.

Baby steps

There are a few ways in which we can begin to open up and let others in on our process. This may be simple for some, but it will be profound for others, so bear with me. I found one of the best mechanisms to share Maddie's Message, and for me to have the opportunity to share with strangers, is that I put Maddie's sweet little face on a random act of kindness card that I could talk about. It's disarming to see a cute little girl on a postcard. Besides, I was able to give them something they could take back home, which encouraged them to spread the message. I didn't know exactly what I was going to do initially, but I knew I needed to do something. I slowly built up to what became the nonprofit, the distribution of the furniture straps, and the act of kindness cards.

A reason why we might want to be open to sharing about our trauma and loss is because we know others may have gone through something similar. In my case, it's to prevent something similar from happening. We're not all that different, and we don't know exactly what's going on inside the minds and hearts of the people in front of us. That's why we need to share. Some days, I consider it a gift that I can tell people about furniture tip-over accidents and help them prevent a disaster from happening to their family. In some unique way, I'm now qualified to share these things. I didn't sign up for this path, but maybe I was chosen. That's how I see it because I'm uniquely qualified to speak in these areas now.

That sense of purpose and identity drives me into small, actionable steps to get the message out. I know it will look different from me to you, and maybe I have a more developed process because I've had some time and help to figure it out. Nevertheless, even if you are on day one of experiencing your trauma and loss, you can start to take baby steps in this area. It's extraordinarily vital to open up and communicate when you're in the grieving phase. We all need to be able to turn to our right or our left and say that we're not okay. We've been traumatized, and we need some help. We need to have the ability and connections to discuss the nuances of our trauma and our healing journey. We can't keep it in. We can't try to deal with it ourselves, because it will only limit our growth and healing.

You may ask yourself how long you need to talk to someone about a trauma or loss that you've experienced. My answer now is a little different than before. We never stop talking about it; the only difference is the subject matter. Rather than me discussing the most painful parts of my trauma and loss, I share the stories from a place of solutions, options, and help. See, I've already processed my pain a million times, and I'm no longer in a state of trauma when I discuss my story. I've transitioned to talk about wisdom and experience, and I try my very best to be a guide to those I speak with. I only got to this place because I started with baby steps. One of the catalysts that helped me open up about my journey was talking to perfect strangers for five seconds in a grocery store line. That repetitive process allowed me to practice on people I didn't know and remove the impossible barriers to thinking about how I can impact the world. Once you've talked to a thousand people in the grocery store line, it's easy to put them in a room and talk to them that way.

You need to define the baby steps that work for you. At a minimum, your goal and plan should be to get back to feeling free with your life and story. If that's the baseline you're setting, that's fantastic. Imagine now, at the end of this goal, that you share enough of your story with enough people and you're no longer held back by feeling inadequate, a lack of confidence, shame, and less than. But you brought yourself back up to normal expectations, and you own your story and your past; it's no longer holding you down, but a part of you. You don't shy away from who you are and what you are about, but you own it and use it in the most positive and optimistic ways. You define the baby steps that work for you, but don't be surprised if you see your goals shift over time. The more you own your story and the more that you share it, the more you will see a transformation that takes place within you, and your actions and behaviors will change accordingly. Your goals will evolve as you own your story—because the more you embrace it, the greater your capacity to achieve bigger and more meaningful milestones. This is what happened to me. I just wanted to set up a website and hoped people would visit it, and now I've helped change legislation. It feels like it's only the beginning, but we must be open to sharing.

Don't feel responsible for their response to your story

The first time I shared my story, I was in trauma. The natural response for me was to try to manage my trauma. This is the case for a majority of people that I share with for the first time. They've never heard this story before, and immediately go to heartfelt sympathy, compassion, and their version of trauma. Maybe you felt this way when you went through the first chapters of this book. Oftentimes, I find myself needing to switch roles from sharing and being a guide to helping them through the trauma that they just experienced by hearing my story.

I was wondering if the trauma they're experiencing now is because of the way that I'm telling the story, or is it just so foreign for them that they're traumatized by the details. I think the details send people into layers of trauma. It became so common that I had to stop my process and my story to comfort them—I realized that, as much as I'd like to be there to support them, it's not my job to manage their response. I would generally stop in the middle and say, "I'm not in a state of trauma right now, so you don't have to be." I think their general sense of love and compassion comes through in how they responded to my story. Still, it's not my intention to bring trauma to someone, and also not my responsibility to manage their reaction to my story.

I learned a few things that may help you as well, because depending on the stories we share and the details we elaborate on, people will be triggered. They'll be traumatized, and you have to understand that this is the first time they're experiencing this level of emotion and detail. They may have a trauma reaction, and that's okay. Let the details be real and known if they are true and authentic. Try to be as sensitive as possible with the different people and environments we connect with. Nevertheless, we can do our best not to over-traumatize them by letting them know the essentials and elaborating when necessary or when asked to.

We must have permission internally to not feel responsible for how others respond to our story and trauma. We have finally drummed up enough courage and confidence to communicate our story. We must realize that everybody will receive our story in a way that matches their perspective and experience. Some will be more traumatized than others. So, what do we do with this information? For starters, we need to be mindful that what we share impacts others, and the goal within our communication should be clear to them. If they're willingly participating, then it's all good. However, suppose we're communicating the deep levels of our trauma and our past to people who are unwilling or not capable of processing these things with us. In that case, we're going to be in damage control mode. We will have to help them through their emotions and thoughts about something we've already processed long ago. We don't want to be in damage control mode because then we feel reserved in sharing our story due to the inability of others to receive it. It's not the story itself that's the problem, it's the person receiving the story—are they capable of processing that level of detail or that kind of trauma? The only thing that we can do is to be mindful of who we share it with and what we share. This includes family members.

The closer someone is to you, the more processing you're going to have to do, and when you experience loss in the family, like I have, it seems that these conversations are either enduring or they never happen. The best thing to do when processing trauma and loss with our family is to let them know where you are, because then they won't drag you down into their process if you're communicating to them that you're much further along. The wellness that comes from this is using communication to lead people to a common goal, rather than venting our frustrations with no objectives. The simplicity of a goal within a conversation with a relative will change everything about how we communicate with them. Don't get me wrong, I'm not saying that you need to have an agenda where you're trying to persuade them or mislead them. I'm saying that if you have an internalized goal that you're communicating to them about going through the stages of healing and processing our experiences in a proactive manner that leads us to wellness, then we're all getting to a better place at the end of the conversation, rather than going around in circles.

Open to feedback

The whole point in us opening up and sharing our process is that we can get feedback. We know that not every person is qualified to give us relational advice, marital advice, or trauma therapy, but their feedback does matter. On a personal level, just being able to process and receive feedback is essential for our relationships. We don't have to do anything with the feedback, especially if it's not pertinent or damaging, but we must be open to hearing it. People want to be listened to, and because they're in our lives, we allow them to speak into our process and journey.

Feedback is vital, not just optional, regarding our healing journey and the experts we brought along the way to help us. There's a process and a procedure that many have studied and perfected, and in which they have tremendous amounts of experience. If we're open to listening to them and taking their feedback to heart, then we can change faster and accomplish the goals that are in our hearts. Who do you have speaking to in your process right now? A few people come to mind whom I've allowed to speak into my life regularly. It doesn't necessarily need to be someone you're in an active relationship with. It's Bobby Bones, Amy Brown, and Mel Robbins. I listen to their shows, their podcasts, and read their books. The feedback that I received, of course, is generally because I'm not in an active relationship with them, but it's vital for them to speak into my process. I have others around me that I can let in on the details of my journey and have them speak into the intimate details of my life.

If I'm not open to hearing feedback, I've leveled off in my growth. If I'm not willing to listen to what others have to say, then why should they listen to what I have to say? Sharing our story, and listening to and hearing feedback, is vital for our short-term and long-term growth. Not only do we want to have people in our lives who are casting vision and speaking from the depths of wisdom and understanding, but we also want to have intimate conversations where we can get feedback from the people we love and know very dearly. This is all vital, and it's easy to see when someone can't receive feedback because the way they act is like they're on an island. Their emotions are on an island, their behaviors are on an island, and they sure have developed a form of isolation because they're alone with their thoughts. We don't want that for ourselves, so I need to be open to feedback. Feedback is not fact. Feedback is neutral and is given out of love!

The vision of the future

There's a beauty, opportunity, and refinement that comes from sharing. Not only are we perfected because we're sharpening each other's skills and refining the rough edges of our process to make them smooth, but we're integrated into a collective vision for our future. Unknowingly, I reached out to the group of parents who had gone through child tip-over accidents, and I wasn't fully aware where our connection could go. Initially, I thought having a common conversation and purpose would be helpful for my healing, but through that time of connection, a vision emerged.

Every time we reached out to each other, conversing on the small and minute details of our process in our lives, not only did we come together for each other, support each other, create a safe space for us to communicate, but we also painted a picture of hope and opportunity through the loss we had just experienced. We saw something with one another and within the opportunity that was before us, and this was only possible because we were open to sharing our journey. We don't know where our story will go. Will it go to the ends of the Earth and transform thousands of lives? Will it modify behavior, save lives, and prevent accidents? We don't know, but just because we don't know doesn't mean we shouldn't participate in the most powerful opportunity that's available to us, which is to share our story.

You may not have a vision yet for where your story can go, but I encourage you to use your voice in as many ways as possible to find freedom, contentment, solace, health, and life. I hope you will find a way to communicate that will unlock you, your opportunity, and your potential in ways you would never imagine happening. I hope you can see the purpose in sharing your story, grab hold of it, perfect it, and let other people in every day because you're worth it and have something to say that could change their life.

CHAPTER 11

DECIDING WHAT TO DO WITH MY PAIN

After the shock and numbness comes the pain in the majority of both physical injuries and emotional losses. We all know what physical and emotional pain feels like. When you fall down, twist your ankle, it hurts, and the pain reminds us there's a problem. The pain is not the problem, but rather the messed-up ankle is. The pain is simply a message telling us that something is wrong. Many times, people get mad at the pain and blame the pain for the message that it sends. Of course, this doesn't solve the pain's message; it just creates a cycle of repetition. The pain sends a message to the brain that says your ankles hurt, and we get mad at the pain for sending the message. See the problem? This practical example happens all the time with our emotional health. When we experience something that's traumatic and wounding with our emotional self, we tell our pain to go away, be quiet, and leave us alone. This obviously doesn't do us very much good.

We need to look at the bedrock of the pain and find ways to resolve the message it's sending us. This doesn't mean we need to dissect how and why we got hurt and why the world would do this to us. It simply means that we need to identify the present tangible cause of our pain. If our ankle hurts, then let's look at ways to improve the stability, inflammation, and strength of our ankle. We all understand this practically because we've been injured in life in major or minor ways. But this analogy goes deep into the mental and emotional side of ourselves. Anytime we feel emotional pain, we need to have a process to address it and resolve it; if not, then it just lingers.

Pain levels change, and it reminds us of our greatest needs

There is a really interesting thing that happens when pain is introduced. In one way, it reminds us of our greatest need at the moment. It's screaming at us, telling us it needs all our attention. This abrupt reality, in essence, forces us to pause our lives and make a momentary change to address the need for the pain. There are very few emotions and feelings that have such a drastic response. Regardless of what we're doing with our lives, the pain now forces us to change momentarily or for the rest of our lives. One of the things that is introduced with the pain is a subconscious understanding of our value systems and our greatest need. It's like we cycle through the thoughts in our mind, heart, and soul simultaneously, asking ourselves what the most important thing is right now. It helps us hone in like a drug to find tunnel vision for what we need most. Our bodies' ability to respond to pain is pretty remarkable, and we should glean from our natural response and emulate its pattern in our mindsets.

Now that we're toying around with the idea of the pain we're feeling being useful to us, let's consider the opportunity we're now presented with. Perhaps we were going through our mundane lives and thought everything was fine, but we were in a hamster wheel of just getting by or not living life to the fullest. Then pain found its way on the scene and stopped us in our tracks. It reminded us that not only is the current situation not okay, and it requires all of our attention, but the life we were living isn't exactly what we would view as picture perfect. There are things we can do differently now to make life better. The pain helped us evaluate the values that we have and the things that we care about. Moreover, the pain that has endured has scared us in unchangeable ways. Those scars are meant to be a daily reminder of what we endured and what we desire to prevent. Anytime someone asks, we can show them our scars because we live with them proudly.

Little did we know that the pain that was introduced would change the course of our lives. One moment at a time, if we look back on when the pain first emerged, our daily choices in our thoughts are now going in a completely different direction. Based on our mindsets, the direction we're going is either an extremely positive or an extremely negative one, but nevertheless, we are not the person we were before. Pain did this to us. Although we may never think it, it has shaped and molded us in ways that some would say are beneficial. It opened our eyes to the possibilities we could not have imagined. It has changed our perspective about the people around us and our desire to care and love them better. It has reminded us daily of our fine, fragile sense of self and how valuable life is.

Now that we get to see our greatest need very clearly and have a renewed perspective of how we can do better and what we can accomplish, let us see how we could work with the pain that we feel to accomplish the greater things in life, because it has revealed these things to us. It forced us to change. How can we partner with the pain we feel to convert it in a way that brings the most benefit to ourselves and those we love? Rather than trying to avoid it, hide it, and run away from it. How about we use the most powerful motivating force next to love to get us all the things in our hearts? Let's put our pain to work.

Take action

You alone have the opportunity to change the course of your life. Either you're committed to keeping the current feelings alive regardless of how good they are for you, or you are willing to change. As much as we'd like to hide behind the excuses and feelings we have just to keep us where we're at, we need to look forward to our goals and create a future and a hope that we can work towards. This isn't just one time in life, like after we've experienced tremendous loss and trauma. This reality is a continuation of the decisions that we need to make every day. Why? It's because the emotional pain often doesn't heal as fast as the physical wounds do. Our emotions are something that we create. And every day, we can create new emotions around the pain we've endured. Do you see the perpetual cycle that can happen here? If the emotional pain presents itself continuously throughout our lives, then we will be permanently traumatized. So, how do we get out of it? The only way we can move forward is by addressing our pain and taking action.

One of the more common misconceptions is that the pain will take care of itself. If we forget about it, it won't be here anymore. We all know where that's going. The pain just finds its way in the future and presents itself at the least opportune time when we feel like we've got it all together, or worse off, when we don't have it together. That's no way to address the pain. Ice cream doesn't take care of it, vacations don't solve it, and new purchases don't buy it away. The pain is still there, and we must confront it head-on with the necessary tools and compassion to answer its cry.

Why is it so important? Not only is it a quality of life issue because we end up walking around self-medicating because of emotional pain, but we also diminish the relationships that are around us because of the burden that we feel internally. Our conversations and demeanor change, and our behaviors change for the worse. The stats aren't very helpful in this situation because some people—with tremendous emotional burdens that are unsolved and unmet—end up making decisions about their lives that have unbelievable consequences. We don't want our family to have to plan more funerals because we never dealt with the emotional pain that we had.

Taking action, simply put, is deciding that you don't like the emotional pain that you're experiencing and that you're willing to be open to a process that assists you with that pain. It may not be black and white where you can sign up for a program or a process and have a result within 90 days. Every person is going to be completely different when it comes to how they process their emotional pain. We may encounter the same trauma and have a different healing journey. Because it may take some time, we need to be patient with ourselves, but time helps us change our perspective about how long ago the situation was. We actually need to take action to resolve our feelings.

Don't ignore your feelings

I'm as guilty as this one as anybody. Anytime I have a strong feeling come up, and find a way to stuff it, I'd be the first to say that doesn't help. When our emotions are talking to us, we need to respond to them. We respond in two ways. We discover why the emotion is talking to us and what it says. We take that information and understand that it's communicating something we might need to listen to. This is when we take action on those feelings. Perhaps the emotion is communicating something from the past or our trauma, and it has nothing to do with the real situation that we're in. This understanding allows us to properly address the emotion we're feeling and not place it in situations that don't belong. The second thing we can do when we have an emotion that pops up is to address it and decide if we want to work with it. When we do this, we say we have an emotion, and it's communicating something to us, but we decide that we don't like that emotion anymore, so we need to change our mindset to produce new emotions. Both of these options are very good because they allow us to use our strong emotions.

If we realize that we're continually being fed a certain feeling, we should ask ourselves if we've addressed the root of that trauma or experience. If it's a repetitive feeling or emotion we don't want to have anymore, then we need to focus on new mindsets that will unlock our new emotions. For instance, in another chapter, we discuss how to take a loss and turn it into something good. This mindset will allow us to flip each strong emotional feeling on its head because now we can use those feelings to benefit our current life.

Our feelings are the first thing we speak up about when something's off. If we think about it from the perspective of being a parent and having kids, we see how vital it is to communicate our feelings and emotions. When your kid comes up to you and says they're angry, don't you want to know where that feeling came from? When they say they're sad, don't you want to know why they're sad? Of course, every good parent would. When we answer our feelings and emotions, even if they're strong ones, we open up a healthy communication cycle to improve the well-being of ourselves and those around us.

Many of us probably grew up in homes where strong emotions could not be communicated. They were either shunned from being talked about, or quickly discarded because they don't make us feel good. We are taught in school that happy and joyful feelings are accepted, but anger and frustration are not permitted. This creates confusion around our emotions and what they tell us, because we're told not to act on certain emotions or talk about them. So we bottle them up, and through the years, we get good at this and become masters at hiding our emotions. What good do you think that does for our spouse and our future relationships? It's not very helpful if you're wondering.

Speaking about our feelings and emotions sets us up to have open and honest conversations. Sometimes we don't have an answer for our feelings; sometimes they're hormonal, sometimes they're chemically based in our mind, and sometimes our body is telling us things, and we don't know why. But let us not be scared to talk about our feelings and emotions with those we love, and ourselves. We never want to have a situation where we keep them inside and hide the truth of what we feel from those we love, and our life and our relationships suffer because of our indecision. Your feelings and emotions are important; you should talk to someone about them. Talk to someone on the merits of sharing, and maybe you'll be able to resolve some of them as well.

Prioritize your well-being

It's hard to know when all the red lights and the warning signs are going off in the dashboard of our mind. Sometimes we just feel like we're pushing through life, and it's just another day, even though we continually see the red flags present themselves. Not only do we want to get the help we need when we need it, but we want to develop a system and a process so we can actively pursue and prioritize our well-being, so we don't have to wait for moments of crisis to seek healthiness. Many people wait until something traumatic happens before they reach out and seek advice and get help. Why not prioritize your well-being now, properly position yourself, and equip yourself to be at peace, content, and healthy? Why not prioritize thriving and your longevity today? I know what you're thinking. It's about time and money, and therefore, that's the reason why you've always pushed it off. But what if it wasn't about time and money, and it was just about prioritizing the right things in life, realizing how important you are, and the value you have for yourself, and making your well-being the ultimate priority alongside those you care for.

Oftentimes, we're convinced to do something not because of what it could bring us but because of what we could lose. If you can't convince yourself to prioritize your health, mind, and peace for the simple benefits of those things transpiring in your life, then let's think about what you could lose. Your life will be cut short if you're no longer here. The people you love so much that you will do anything for will no longer have that person in their life. They will lose all of you because you do not prioritize your well-being. We all know why you feel the way that you feel, and you're justified in feeling that way, but at some point, the decision to not prioritize your health is yours.

There may be another way to discuss it, and I always remind myself of this. I see the value itself in improvement and self-development. If I put forth a decent effort and pursue it as a competition, I will see good results in my work and life. So I've started prioritizing my well-being, simply because I need to conquer and accomplish this. That pursuit for me was everything because I like tackling things, I like accomplishing things, and the drive and the motivation to conquer and prove others wrong drives me to do great things, even if those great things mean taking care of myself. So I utilize the pursuit to position my care and well-being properly.

I've got to admit I'm not the best at this, but I'm aware of the necessity, and I'm constantly looking for ways to improve my process, because I know people depend on me, and it's worth trying. I realize that the more I participate in well-being exercises, the more I see value within myself. And the more I care about myself, the more I will prioritize my short-term and long-term well-being. It's not hard to do; we just need to prioritize it. On the weekend, go on short walks, practice breathing exercises, or work out. Some people get a lot out of making a meal for themselves, watching a movie, or reading a book. There's no right or wrong answer when prioritizing your well-being. The only way that we miss it is if we neglect ourselves and the needs that we have.

Mental health is vital

Our minds are the gates for our experience in life. They set the precedence for everything that we perceive and how we behave. Most of us have gone to the doctor and gotten blood work done. The doctor tells us whether or not we're healthy or need some work or medication. The visit is more or less a report card on the health of our body. We all understand that process and what it leads to in making better decisions for our physical body. But there are very few such examples that we have when it comes to our Mental Health. There are a lot of people who have pioneered mental health over the years, and in the self-help environment, we have seen tremendous help emerge over the last decade. The need is evident, and there have been individuals who have pioneered these conversations more recently. Jelly Roll and many other emerging artists have talked about their struggle and pain in the process that they've gone through to talk about their feelings and concerns with their loved ones, and those around them to support them. We can't have too many people sharing their stories and talking about their struggles and where they find victory.

The internal battles we face in our minds are not something we should face alone. We need to let others into our thoughts. Some days are easier than others. Some days, we wake up with thoughts like mini-tornadoes, and we cycle through every option under the sun—we entertain many thoughts that aren't helpful to us. This may be normal to experience, but it's also a sure tell sign of someone who needs tools and resources to ensure that their mental health is a priority. I'm not an expert by any means, but I'm aware of the need. So I ask you, what are you doing today to prioritize your mental health? If you feel your response is inadequate to your needs, you should act on that. We know ourselves better than anybody knows us. If you feel like you lack in this area, look at yourself in the mirror and get help. The help doesn't need to be expensive either. You can start by listening to audiobooks, podcasts, and radio shows. There are an amazing number of people on YouTube and online who are offering free advice every day.

We just have to put forth the effort once we see the need. Honestly, it doesn't matter if you're male or female, we all have the same needs in terms of our mental health. One shouldn't avoid getting help because they're too prideful to ask for help. Pride is something you build by realizing your strengths and weaknesses, maximizing your efforts for the betterment of yourself and the people around you. You can be proud of that, not about keeping secrets and then crashing and burning. There's no pride in our destruction.

Everybody should consider investing in themselves, and this could cover a multitude of things, including our mental development. Take a small amount of time and money, and position it in a way that supports your development. This means attending conferences, training, counseling, and coaching. You can pay for one hour of somebody's time and they could change the course of your life for 10 years. We don't need to do this alone, and the world's big enough a place where we can find the resources that we need.

The small steps bring us the most progress, and we just need to apply ourselves to the lifestyle of development and progression. For me, I feel like it's been seasonal. I've been able to apply myself to my personal development more in certain seasons than others, but if I sense that there's a need, I lean into it. Sometimes it takes the loving nudges of the people around us to force us to get help. I say bring it on because at the end of the day, making ourselves better for those around us also puts them in a better place. So, what will you commit to that would bring you health and longevity in your mind? Make it simple and practical so that you can see the progress. I'm thankful I was nudged into the Emotional Intelligence Leadership training course I have just recently finished. Life-changing is an understatement. I've learned and grown more just this year with the tools and coaching provided here. (www.nextleveltrainings.com)

Let's not forget our environment. Our environment is a pivotal component of our overall well-being. The data shows that the more integrated we are with our communities, the better off our mental health will be. This means that having friends and a normal social life is vital for mental health. We'll find an outlet that will allow us to voice our general concerns before they become level 4 dumpster fire concerns, and people who care. I hope that you've been able to experience the love and care that comes from those around you when you're in a time of need—it's an unbelievable feeling to lean on others when the need is the greatest.

Put your pain to work

In life, we always seek inspiration or a reason to do something. We've been looking for a new tool for a long time to get us from where we're at now to where we're going, but we didn't know that we had everything available at our fingertips to get us going. We all have pain and unspent frustration. Why don't we convert that pain we feel and allow it to accelerate our lives instead of pulling us down? Why don't we think of pain as a tool that motivates us rather than hinders us? What could we accomplish if we converted our pain into something useful that wakes us up in the morning and excites us every day?

It will take everything we have to convert this pain into a usable resource for ourselves, but what other options do we have? Shall we sit around and enjoy the pain a bit more because we don't know it as well as we thought we did? Forget that. Instead of wallowing in my misery, I prefer to use this pain as a primary source of my motivation. What if we let our pain be our primary source of motivation in this next season? I'm not saying it has to be for every season, because we don't need it to be. Perhaps other seasons are filled with a pursuit of happiness and satisfaction, rather than pain, which is a primary motivator.

What if we allowed our pain to push us into greatness, and used it as a tool to guide us toward our goals and ambitions? We don't want to waste our pain because it's the fuel to get us to our next milestone, and we've already felt it, so why not convert this into energy? Our ambitions don't need to be grandiose; they just need to be practical. With one small step at a time, we can accomplish great things.

Every single day, we're given the option to direct our lives and decide what motivates us. If we set in our hearts that we're going to use the things that were meant to pull us down and convert them into energy to push us forward, then what can stop us? Anytime we're looking for a little motivation, we should check back in with the pain we felt and see how we can prevent that from happening to someone else. We may make up the time and the loss by what we accomplish. I remember when I started on this journey, the first positive use of my pain was to get out of bed and do something with it, when everything inside of me didn't want to. I knew that my family would be better for it if I did. Maybe that is your goal today, just to get out of bed. You rise because you have a life to live, a story to tell, wonderful things to accomplish, and people to help. Let pain be one of the greatest motivators that you've ever been given.

12

CHAPTER

GOOD THINGS DO
COME FROM LOSS

I was given two options when I encountered the loss of three very close family members. Either I perceive their loss as lives stolen from me, and there's nothing to gain from this experience, or I can find some redemptive value.

I knew this wasn't just a self-soothing exercise to make myself feel better. After I got the donor call and I found out that Maddie's life was shared to help others live a full, complete life, I realized that good things can come out of loss. There is redemptive value in it. Of course, the mother and human side of me says, "You know, it's just tremendous pain, and what good was it? Why would this happen to people I love?" Rational thoughts and logical explanations don't suffice for loss and trauma. We don't have the answers to why we always experience loss. We may inherently know why. Like, I know my daughter died from a furniture tip-over accident, but why did she have to die? Why did it have to be her? My spiritual and emotional side will never understand all the reasons, so I'm left with the two options I presented to you. Either I'm a permanent victim, or I will try to find some good in this.

I fight and contend to try to find the good in these terrible situations because I want to make sure that I value to the best of my ability the sacrifice that was made, or the loss of life that happened. If I don't see value in it, then it doesn't matter. The loss, pain, and trauma don't matter. But if I value those who gave their life, and I care about their legacy and their sacrifice and contribution, then that value is extended in my efforts to find good in these terrible situations. Because I love them, I don't have a choice but to see all the bad, I have to find the good, and sometimes that good is placed in their life, and what they could give to those around them, like my nephew and my brother. They gave us wonderful experiences, joyful moments, companionship, laughter, and fun when they were with us. I treasure those moments and see how valuable they are and how they can be even still to this day. I can think back on laughing with my brother and hanging out with my nephew, which brings me delight and joy. Their lives continually give more and more because I have taken a position to think about the redemptive moments.

Because if you think about it, the only thing we have left of them is our memories, and why would we disregard all the good memories and only think about the bad ones? Our view of the people we've loved and lost should be of every good thing they gave us. It's that relationship with our memories and perspective that we need to protect to ensure their life and legacy have value and meaning for us today. You can make it as intentional as you want to be. It doesn't take long for every person that I meet to find out about Maddie and what she's done for me and others. It's a joy and a delight for me to go out and share her message with strangers. That doesn't happen naturally. I have to work hard, guarding my heart and my mind, so that I can be as productive as possible with my actions and perspective.

Our development

For some people, this exercise may be hard because maybe you may have experienced a loss and trauma, and the memories you have aren't so fun and cherished. This is the case all the time for people who are abused and mistreated. The redemptive moments may come from our process and our journey. Oftentimes, the battle and the season of trauma and struggle are so great that our journey of overcoming the struggle, the emotional turmoil, and the situational trauma is our redemptive path. Not only can we discover things within ourselves, such as resilience, grit, fortitude, strength, compassion, understanding, and love—we can also develop a new path and a new plan for our life because we have experienced this trauma and loss.

We are the testament of surviving and finding a way to thrive after having experienced such evil things. We may not be able to find any good in those who have harmed us, but we can see the good that's developed within us, and perhaps we can impart some of that to those around us in ways that we find fitting. Even though we may have experienced pure evil, we don't want to waste it. Uniquely, we are qualified based on trial and error to assist others and help them overcome what we've endured. Not only can we take the overwhelming resistance and allow it to develop us internally like channeling all of that anger and hatred and bitterness and resentment into developing a skill or learning something new. The process of strengthening and building moments in a lifestyle of resilience is always something that we should be grateful for because no one can take that away from us. Not only will we become unstoppable in some areas as we look back and see the progress we've made, but we will also be able to push down the other obstacles in our lives with ease because of our newfound strength and resilience.

Many people turn to a self-mastery and self-development journey when they've experienced the depths of trauma. They can apply themselves to physical development by working out and improving their image. This, of course, means changing and modifying food consumption through better choices and moderation. Something about the internal development matches the physical image that we see in the mirror, and that is so transformative. Again, once you get healthy, nobody can take that away from you.

What are some ways you can take your pain and frustration, your uncertainties, your failures, and your emotions and put them to work for you? It doesn't necessarily need to be in the same vein in which your feelings have transpired. If you've experienced loss or trauma, you can channel the strong emotional feelings that you have into developing a skill or a new routine in life that serves you better. Even if they're small micro-changes you've committed to making now to better yourself and those around you, it's worth it. I know many people who have lost loved ones due to alcoholism and drugs. Perhaps it's a good idea to implement a plan and a course of action so that you and your current loved ones don't experience that same loss by simply setting a standard, setting a curfew, knowing our limits, and asking for help. These are very effective ways to channel the loss we've experienced into the future good.

The hardest part for some people is finding out what they want to pursue. When we've experienced overwhelming and tremendously difficult things in life, it's hard not to stare at the elephant in the room. After we experience such loss, how could we not focus on the loss that we've experienced? Slowly and surely over time, as we begin our healing process and embrace our newfound realities, we can start to see a clear picture for ourselves of what we could be, who we can become, and what we're supposed to do with our lives now. All of this forward-thinking doesn't happen instantly; sometimes it just happens naturally. Some people were introduced into my life during my moments of trauma that have been there for me ever since and helped shape the course of what I do regularly. I didn't know them before, and I didn't know how to reach out to them before, but it happened naturally. We've got to be open to that. People falling into our laps, and we don't understand it, apart from thinking maybe God sent them. We need these people to help us see the good that we want to pursue, because it is so easy to focus on the negative and focus on the strong emotions and ignore the purpose and the goal in our efforts.

I found a lot of healing in doing things for others. Some people might find a tremendous amount of healing before they start reaching out and making themselves available to the world again. For myself, I needed to get my mind and body working for a new cause, which jump-started the healing process for me. Not only was I being healed in reaching out and finding satisfaction in the eyes of the people around me, because I knew I was helping them, but they were obviously given the most passionate and connected form of myself that I have presented to the world. There's nothing like experiencing something that dramatically changes you and imparting the best advice to those around you.

If you've noticed one thing in this book, our efforts are not short-lived, and our story shouldn't be either. Everything we do should be a lifestyle of transformation and effect. My actions and efforts may slowly change over time based on the season I'm in and the opportunities in front of me. Still, I am committed to applying myself in my personal development to be the best version of myself today while embracing all of my past.

Some 17 years later, I still sign up for coaching, counseling, conferences, podcast radio shows, and I read constantly. I know I can better myself and use all I have while I'm still here. Not only will those around me benefit tremendously, but I will be able to do things in my life, family, and career that may have seemed impossible before. I like to believe that if we're not moving forward, we are moving backwards. Look through the windshield, not the rearview mirror. This needs to be our framework of understanding as we also see our past. Is my past allowing me to move forward, or is it holding me back? Rather, in what ways can I perceive my past to move me forward instead of holding me back? Did you notice how I turned two options into one ultimate option? Sometimes we must frame our perspective so that only one choice benefits us.

What good can we do now?

One of the beautiful things that has come out of my story is the trajectory of my life, which was molded and shaped by the circumstances I experienced. I thought about helping others more than I could have imagined. As you know, I connected with different groups and established different plans to prevent furniture tip-overs. The main group I connected with in 2019 was formed earlier that year. I found them on Facebook, and their group had nine parents in it who had all lost children the same way that I lost Madison.

Through my efforts and those of the group PAT, we started a nonprofit, and we advocate on behalf of our children. Every time you buy something from IKEA or one of your favorite furniture places, you're going to get some screws and straps and hooks to mount it on the wall. Or even better, you can count on it being built the correct way. We did that! Think of the untold good that came out of our loss.

And, regularly, I make myself available for grief counseling to newly bereaved parents. I'm able to use my education, my experience,

GOOD THINGS DO COME FROM LOSS | 161

and my emotional process to benefit others. To those parents who had just lost a child and some of their organs are being donated, now they're able to talk to me. People like me provide answers to questions, emotional support, companionship, and just someone who will listen and understand the process they are going through. It's hard not to see the good in that. There's so much good in it. My life is rerouted to accommodate this kind of good. I know everyone won't have the same option to apply themselves to a cause because of their loss and trauma, but many incredible organizations do good regularly. I didn't know anything about furniture tip-overs before the accident happened. Now, I consider myself an expert because I've rerouted my life to help end this thing.

For me, turning these negative situations into something good was out of my internal desire to do something about them. I felt ashamed and insignificant, and I was unable to help bring my daughter back. I was internally driven just to do something about my lack of feeling like I had any help or sense of control. Maybe the drive was initially selfish because it was centered around my emotional needs and inadequacies, but ultimately, it was good.

There's beauty in trying to find the good in inherently bad things. I think it's a matter of the heart. Either we want good things to happen, and therefore we will find them, or we don't. Even in the worst possible cases of loss and trauma, we can still find some good, even if it completely relies on the prevention of it happening again. If only we could give ourselves that as the greatest good that could come of such terrible situations. That we prevented this bad thing from happening again, or at least we did our part to prevent it from happening again. How much good is there in that? I believe it's so valuable. It's literally life-changing at a base minimum. And this can be done in an amazing number of ways. Like telling your story, which we've talked about in another chapter. Simply letting people know what happened is a form of help and prevention. It's a beautiful thing. To be clear, I don't feel high and mighty and amazed by all the good work I'm doing. Sometimes I feel like nobody cares, and this effort is pointless. But based on some of the feedback I've been getting, we have helped save lives and prevent future disasters. Sometimes it's impossible to know the full effects of what we've done, but even if one life was saved or one trip to the hospital was prevented, then it was worth it.

Maybe you can find happiness and joy in giving some time to a cause that you find relatable and meaningful. What would that be for you? Could you donate one hour a month or a hundred bucks to something that you see as important? You can give out of the overflow and the bottom of your heart to make these meaningful moments happen. You won't believe the transformation you will receive when you use your heart, mind, and actions to give back. There's a crazy process in our brain that is awakened when we give selflessly for the cause of another. It's one of the most remarkable things that we can participate in regularly. For those who struggle with their emotions and their confidence, the very action of connecting with others solves those emotional needs. Once you've established that you are worth it, you quickly realize that they are too, and so your efforts are invaluable.

Becoming a donor

Although it may be a weird concept when you're standing in the line at the DMV and the person across the counter asks you if you want to donate your organs, yes or no, it's an extremely important one. Let's think about it for a second. If something has happened to you, and the question should come up about your organs, that means you're no longer with us. You're gone and passed away. Your organs are no good to you anymore. They don't serve you in the way they did before because now you're in heaven and your flesh is going to wither away in the dirt. I hate to put it so bluntly. I know that you're personally attached to every one of your organs as they are yours and yours alone, but wouldn't you want to gift the remaining life that you have, including your flesh, to someone in need after you pass?

I understand it may seem weird, and it may take some convincing. Initially, I was open to the idea for myself. I knew that if I were dead, my body would be no good to me anymore, and so I might as well put it to use, right? When the question came up to me in the hospital about my daughter, I didn't even consider it a question at all. The idea that she could live on and her incredible organs and flesh could be used to bring life to other kids in need was absolutely what I wanted to do. When I was faced with this proposition, it seemed like the answer was already made because if I think about it the other way around, and I rejected the donation of her organs, then I would be withholding the very thing that a few kids needed to survive and thrive. I believe that donating our organs and tissue is something that everyone should do. It's the basic human good that we can participate in. Of course, it comes at a tremendous loss, but that loss doesn't need to be in vain. It can be an answer to prayer for someone in need. If you have a child, please consider this a way to bring good to humanity. For yourself, the next time you renew your driver's license, tell them to update that little checkbox on whether or not you're an organ donor. Think about what it means to the people in need. This is one of the most beautiful ways to love the people around us, even when we've experienced loss ourselves. Thank you for considering this.

Our lives are like seeds

We know firsthand that we can't control big areas of our lives. Sometimes life just happens, and we're left with picking up the pieces. Sometimes disappointment and heartache are our best friends for a while. Sometimes loss and pain are too familiar. This leaves us with pure loss. The only thing that we can do with that loss is to plant it. It's essentially a seed in our hands. It died off, and what it was once capable of is no longer. But that doesn't mean that it still doesn't have potential. Every seed carries within itself a promise and a possibility of a future. The seeds' DNA tells a story of a possible hope and a dream. This is the redemptive path and plan for anyone and everyone who has experienced loss.

These hopes and dreams may be different now, but they can definitely birth something great and of tremendous value. This is my perspective on my second daughter, Ellie. She came forth after Maddie died. The seed and desire to have a daughter were planted in my heart, and once that was taken away from me, I seized on the opportunity to have another. I'm grateful for the daughter she is. No one could replace Maddie, but Ellie filled a gaping hole that existed in our family. She brought back joy. She completed our family in a way only she could.

If we're going through life with this mindset in our back pocket, then we can turn our failures into some of the things that we're most proud of. Even our mistakes and the things that we regret can be seeds that allow us to see the possibility of change. Sometimes we don't figure all the pieces out on our own, and we need some jolting trauma and loss to wake us up. If we consider this a moment of reflection or a wake-up call, we're using the things designed to set us back for our good. Do you see where I'm going with this? If even the things designed to destroy us can be used for our good, what stops you? I'm doing the most good, from becoming the best, to changing the world? For goodness' sake, you've already been through hell and back; you might as well make the trip worthwhile. It's time to bring back some souvenirs.

You can't leave God out of the equation

Most people turn to God after they've experienced loss and trauma. There's something about our human nature when it's stripped away, when all of our expectations are gone or crushed—we look to God for help. I did this almost instinctively. God was always an option in our family. Regardless of how much you consider faith a central focal point of your life, you should consider what God could do in the face of your loss. What's the harm in inviting him onto the journey with you? Either you will do it alone, or you might get some assistance.

When we consider the option and the opportunity for God to help us, I think we're open to a realm of possibility that I never imagined before. I can tell you firsthand that situations, events, and encounters with people took me back and surprised me. I felt like there were some heavenly-orchestrated events to help me get back on my feet and to guide the way. I mentioned the twin butterflies that came after my brother's passing to you. That, to me, was the overwhelming feeling and sensation of being loved, embraced, and cared for by God. We need to be open to these moments because loss is so significant and overwhelming that we should be able to take anything to assist us and help us. I find coins all the time, and most especially when I'm having a bad day, or a sad moment, these coins are little reminders to me. I think of them as little gifts from Maddie. Let's put aside our intellectual framework and pride to allow a spiritual process to happen. God is an important part of my life. Although I can't explain everything, and I don't have answers for everything, I believe that he helps me. I can see his handiwork regularly through my partnership with him. If anybody can relate to our pain and loss, it's God, so we might as well have him on our side and look for the good that could come from it. I believe that you'll be better for it, because I know I am.

13

DON'T WISH THAT
YOU WOULD HAVE

I must admit I've had some regrets, and I've also taken note of the regrets that the people around me have had. Not only do I want to pass on some regrets that you can avoid, but I also implore and encourage you to live a life that prioritizes the most valuable things. "Don't wish that you would have," is a phrase that came to me, through my dad, sometime between my daughter's and brother's passing. It was how we tried to express urgency when sharing the dangers of furniture safety. It's become so much more over the last several years as I apply that theory in all areas of my life. So here I am carrying the torch, handing it off to you, saying, please don't have these same regrets. Don't wish that you would have...

Told your story

Don't wish that you had told your story. This one was so important that I dedicated an entire chapter to it. We go through life and encounter hurdles, obstacles, and traumas, but we don't tell anybody about them because we feel we are inconveniencing them or our stories are not worth it. Some of us sit next to the people we profess to love, and they still don't know about what we've endured in our past. Not only are we self-isolating, but we're refusing to be known, and therefore our actions limit our ability to be seen, heard, and loved. The very effort of sharing our story will bring a more positive and responsive connection to those around us.

As communicated throughout this book, I make it a point to open up in both small and big ways. First, I start with my family. The challenging conversations are not off limits, especially when it comes to trauma and loss. I encourage everybody to share their thoughts and I share mine with them. This environment is not always fun because we talk about difficult things, and people share strong emotions. However, a better outcome is hoped for and planned because now my family can speak their mind and hear everyone's thoughts and feelings.

The communication of our story doesn't stop with our family. I plan activities and events with my nonprofit and at work to share my story and journey openly. I make it a habit to plan with our organization through the kindness cards, speaking events, and random encounters at the grocery store to connect with people over Maddie's Message. Sure, it doesn't always feel the best. I'm not always excited about it, but I understand the importance of doing it daily. It's kind of like trying to eat healthy. Sometimes it doesn't feel the best and isn't exciting, but we should do it.

Because this is more of a lifestyle for me, I have always made it a point to share my story.

The way I see it is these perfect strangers may never see me again, but if I have the opportunity to connect with them right now on something that could change their life or their family's life, then why was I given this opportunity to meet them? Moreover, this is the challenging one. It's when we know that we're supposed to be talking to them and helping them, but we refuse to because our feelings got in the way, and we find out later that something happened that was preventable. In my case, I would say a lot of these "quote-unquote" accidents are extremely preventable, and unfortunately, I've heard testimony of situations where the needless loss of life happened because of preventable accidents.

So I ask myself, am I given a choice if I truly care about these people? I don't want to wish I had told my story, nor should you. Your voice and your testimony is one of the most powerful things that you have to use in your life, and if sharing your story saves a life or helps someone then please find the courage to open up every once in awhile—maybe once a week or maybe just one time per day to change the course of history, and to change the lives of those that you love. Say it with me. I will share my story because it's valuable and will help those I love.

Taken the pictures

After I lost Maddie, and during Noah's (my nephew) sickness, it occurred to me that we never got any professional pictures done. This is a regret that I have, and I guess you could say it's lost memories, because our mind and memories are fleeting. We might have an image or a small memory that comes to mind, but we will never know exactly what they look like during that time; we just have a general idea or feeling. Madison's death was unexpected, but with Noah, we had some time to plan. We had those family pictures taken, and I'm so glad we did. There's something to be said for regularly planning professional photos to be done because we don't know what curveballs will take place in life. Everybody gets to dress up, put on a smile, and allow the rest of us to remember them for all the wonderful and good they were, and all the joy they brought us.

I'm thankful for the technology available to us now through our iPhones and Androids, where we can take pictures at any given time, whereas before it was difficult. Perhaps we can prioritize taking family photos regularly in our lives to document the journey of growing up and what we've accomplished. Nobody has any regrets about filling up their camera roll with their family and their experiences. I do know, however, people who regret not taking enough photos when they had the opportunity to. So, don't wish you had taken more photos because when your family members are no longer there, their warmth and presence are not something you can reach for, but a photo of them is.

There are also so many wonderful apps that allow us to document the journey of our lives, and it's so easy to plan these things now. I hope that my regret instills a plan and a prioritization in your life to take more photos, because that's something that you can do now proactively to enjoy the moments and relive those moments. After all, you are intentional and live a life of no regrets. The only way to live without regret for your life is to plan it that way. Don't wish you had taken more photos of those you love.

Taking care of yourself

When it comes to our health and well-being, we can redo only so many things. Not every process and every outcome is reversible, and we only have one of us in this beautiful experiment of life. So why would we neglect taking care of ourselves if we don't have a second chance at life? Have we been convinced of the excuses on why we should neglect our health and push aside things that truly matter for things that don't? It's apparent to me that life's demands and our unique desire to serve others put us in a position to neglect ourselves regularly. As justifiable as it may seem, we still agree to neglect our own needs, which isn't a desired outcome that anybody truly wants. This is something I remind myself of all the time. Life can get away from us, and one crisis goes into the next, or one busy season goes into the next, and before you know it, we have neglected ourselves.

That's life, right? But it doesn't have to be. It simply comes down to the things that we prioritize, what we plan for, and what we don't. Studies show that the more we plan and write things down, the more likely they will happen, because desire and action are very different. If we desire to be healthy and live long, we must also plan for our health and long life. This doesn't surprise you, but it's a reminder not to regret the things you truly care about and value the most. We don't get second chances when it comes to prioritizing our health. Some people abuse their bodies, thinking that they're invincible, perhaps because of age.

I know our younger selves didn't feel like anything bad would happen to us or that we would die. Of course, this is an easy fallacy because life happens and gets away from us. Aside from the surprises of life, the things that we can plan are the things that we should take hold of. Our life, our health, and our overall well-being are things that we largely can't control. When you have a conversation with yourself or someone you know, the number one regret is that they wish they had been healthier, worked out more, eaten less, or treated themselves more to healthy activities and exercises. The best day to make the changes was yesterday, but today is the second-best day. Let's dream for a second, if you were to put together a plan for your well-being that had no limitations to it, so you could not only preserve your life but get the most out of life because your health and your longevity do not limit you, what would that plan entail? Would it involve drinking less alcohol, working out a little more, eating one less dessert, or going on more walks? What would you do differently today if you could choose to bring yourself a thriving life?

The most exciting thing about this question is that our responses and reasoning no longer have to wait. Our lives are not so busy that we can't work in 10 or 15 minutes on the things we need to take care of ourselves. There's no real reason why we can't prioritize our well-being today in small and impactful ways. The only thing holding us back was feeling the overwhelming need of the season and getting distracted from the ultimate goals that bring us health and life. We don't want to wish that we had taken care of ourselves.

Why would we prioritize our health and wholeness and not have any regrets? It's because we want to live and be around for a long time. We want to share so many wonderful memories with our partner. We want to see our kids and their grandkids grow up. Lastly, we want to do everything that's in our heart to do, and we can't do it if we're not healthy and whole.

Moment by moment, it's hard to see the effects of our decisions because we can't yet measure whether or not a decision was good or bad. However, over time, we can see very clearly the patterns and progress our decisions have made. Either we eat healthy and work out, and you can see the progress in our bodies, or we have some weight to lose. This is a gentle reminder to measure our decisions and not feel too far gone. Every day is a day that we can choose to live a different life and improve by 1%. These micro-decisions will accumulate in a life according to one's desires. I just hope your desire involves not having any regrets about caring for yourself. This includes your body, soul, mind, and emotions. Don't wish that you had taken care of yourself.

Own your career decisions

I've been working diligently since I was 16, and I couldn't have been happier with being so determined about work. So many people feel like their career path and job are not something they can control early on. Some of us are given directives from our family and friends in pursuing certain career paths. We just go with the flow because we don't have a preference or need money. It's rather funny that we care so much about the kind of ice cream we eat, and some people don't care much about where they spend 8 to 10 hours daily.

Our career paths and the choices that we make within our career have vital importance to the trajectory of our success, the amount of time that we will be able to spend with our family, how much money we're going to make, stress, the limitations within our schedule, etc. I can't stress enough how important it is to own your career decisions from consideration through to what you actually apply to what you build on your own. If you have goals and aspirations of spending most of your time with your family at home, then you must build a career path or partner with one that allows it. Rather than just saying yes to the next gig, what is your ideal situation, and what are your goals and values?

There are several stages of my career trajectory that I was really happy to make. I saw what I wanted and worked hard to make that happen. If we do all this work and ensure our lives are healthy, we've taken care of our emotional past. We've built up resilience to overcome the obstacles in life, and we don't take responsibility for our career decisions, so it feels like we're missing the mark.

Maybe you're in a job or career you know is not for you. Then perhaps every day that you stay there not only keeps you from fulfilling your heart's desire and bringing about the success and thriving possibilities of what's available to you, but you also have to endure a day in a less-than-experience. It's really good to sort the hobbies from the career paths because some people get confused. The reward from taking ownership of our career path is incredible. Not only is it something you get to take with you because you own it, but it will also leave you with no regrets. And I feel like, at this point so far in my life, I've largely not had any regrets about my chosen career path.

I understand how important it is. Not only do you have the financial well-being of yourself and your family to consider, but you also spend more time at work than in most places. We have to enjoy what we do, and we have to develop skills that are transferable and that we feel like we're good at. You and you alone will be working this job, so why would you allow anybody else to alter those decisions for yourself? You will see the reward
of your efforts, so why not work on something you're happy about and proud of?

Don't wish you had made different career choices. Make them now. Sometimes, a little overlap and planning are necessary to make these transitions happen, but they're not impossible. If you were to look at yourself in the mirror today and think of the career path that you've chosen, what would you do differently? What would your goals and aspirations be in your chosen career? If you're coming up with a different answer than the one you're currently on, it's time to get to work. Remember, you're worth it, and you should live a life without regrets. You will be happier, and your goals will be fulfilled more regularly. Don't leave your career path to someone else who controls your destiny. Oftentimes, we're just disappointed with the lack of care and results at some point when other people are responsible for our financial well-being. Don't wish that you had taken ownership of your career choices.

Anchor your furniture

Of course, I can't write this whole book and not implore that you anchor your furniture one last time. I believe deeply in the prevention of certain situations from happening. I know deep down inside that Maddie's life didn't need to be lost to something preventable, along with all the other kids who are affected by this annually. It's so easy to reach out to organizations like ours, and we'll supply you with free furniture straps if you don't have them or cannot access them somewhere. (www. maddiesmessage.com)

If you're a parent, there shouldn't be a question about whether or not you want to anchor your furniture. And if you're getting the straps for free, it shouldn't be a question of affordability either. It comes down to your willingness to see the value within your little kids' lives and take 20 minutes to anchor your furniture to the wall. I hate to put it bluntly, but we do what we value. And now, because you know your loose furniture is a hazard to your little ones, you should put a call to action on your calendar to work on this as soon as possible. I know it's inconvenient, but wouldn't you prefer this minor inconvenience over attending an unexpected funeral? As my son Tyler puts it, "I'd rather put a hole in the wall than have to put a hole in the ground." Of course, you would. Thank you for allowing me to communicate the importance of this to you, and I hope you take action to prevent these preventable accidents.

If you're a grandparent, then the same scenario applies to you. If those grandkids come over and start pulling on stuff one second when we're not watching, it could be a bad outcome, and I also offer free furniture straps for all grandparents. Sometimes our kids are so busy that we need to help them with these things that matter, so please pick up the responsibility of ensuring that your furniture is anchored to the wall, and your kids' furniture is anchored to the wall. We know everybody's busy, especially being a new parent, so the next time you have a conversation with your kids, bring this up and make sure that they're taken care of, so you don't have any regrets.

If you read this book and you know someone who needs this information, it's your job to share it. Share it with everyone. Please, Don't wish you would have.

Preventing the preventable

As parents, we all have a list of things we know we must do to protect our family and keep our kids safe. Maybe it's fixing something we put off, like the springs on the trampoline need to be replaced, or some electrical outlets need covers. Life has gotten away from us, and we feel like we've been too busy to slow down and take care of the things we need to do. After a quick reminder of what we truly care about, we should put a plan into action to ensure we do everything in our power to prevent the preventable. I'm telling you this now because I stared at that dresser the night before it took my daughter's life. I don't want that to be you, and it doesn't have to be.

Every season of life has its challenges and cautionary events. Take a few minutes to research the things you should be aware of and should put in measures of prevention within each year of your child's life. Oftentimes, it's not just the emergency room list and the top five causes of injury and death. It's researching ways to baby-proof your home and how to prevent common injuries and illnesses from happening to your child. If you just do a quick Google search, you'll find out there are a tremendous number of preventable trips to the ER and a definite loss of life.

I know this may seem like homework, but isn't it worth it if you can do something today or put in a little effort every couple of months to rule out all the preventable accidents? Your family will appreciate your overwhelming care and devotion to their well-being. In the moment when you're screwing your furniture into the wall and you're fixing something that could cause harm it just feels like work but once it's done you can enjoy the life that you preserved and you got to watch grow up. Do your part and prevent the preventable for your family's well-being.

The future you

Take this book as a beautiful reset. Now you have the opportunity to take everything that's been thrown at you, everything you've experienced, and any loss and trauma that you felt—you can make it work for you, and you can make the best of it. Allow this time to explore the new version of you. Perhaps you've already put so much of what we've discussed in this book to work. You may be ready to turn the page to the new chapter of your life. We don't forget the loved ones that we've lost and the pain that we've endured; rather, we love them willingly every single day by pushing forward.

I applaud your persistence and resiliency up to this point. You've made it this far, which speaks volumes to your care, heart, love, and devotion. Perhaps you feel like you could be better and more resilient moving forward. Well, take this as a wonderful opportunity to start over or to build on what you've already created. Even the mistakes we've made and the times we've missed it are not in vain. They've trained and educated us on how to respond when we are in moments of survival and serious trials. We can't consider it all a loss. The only thing we can do is take our past and rebound, reflect, reinforce, reimagine, and bring resolve.

When you look at yourself in the mirror now, you should consider who you could become versus who you saw yourself as. Rather than holding your image up against your past self, consider what it would be like to hold yourself to the standard of the best possible version of you. Not only are you fully equipped to take the next steps in that direction, but no one's holding you back but yourself. The stories and experiences, including all the bad ones, can fuel your fire to motivate you, change you, and perfect you into the person you are meant to be.

Have you ever thought that the experiences and the stories that you have are uniquely qualified to help someone else around you? It's true. You could be the key to someone's future if you make yourself available to them, whether by sharing your message, your story, or creating a moment of excellence or compassion. You have deep down inside of you what the world needs. And the only way for that to be unlocked is for you to remain resilient in all that you do. You have to take life's resistance and tension as a tool to overcome. We have to turn our pain into purpose, and we have to turn our loss into seeds that are planted for our future.

Regardless of whatever comes our way, staying resilient will allow us to come out the other side, be victorious, and have no regrets. Imagine with me for a moment what you could create with no regrets. Suppose you took every obstacle coming your way as an opportunity to build yourself, become a better person, become stronger, and become wiser. What could stop you from becoming the best mom, dad, brother, sister, spouse, coworker, and friend?

Little reminders

I leave you with a modified kindness card. As I told you once before, I have these cards with my little girl's face on them, and they're passed out as an initiative for people to display random acts of kindness. Perhaps they buy somebody's coffee behind them in the coffee line or help somebody move their furniture. These random acts of kindness open up people's hearts and minds, and hopefully move them by the kindness in a way that they want to reproduce it. I hope this book was a random act of kindness to you. I hope that it helped you understand yourself better. I hope you'll find so much value within yourself now that you can't help but give it away, just as I have in these pages.

Regardless of what you may encounter in the days ahead, you can set yourself up with little reminders of why you're doing what you're doing. You can look down on those little pigtails and remember why you must remain resilient. You can feel that presence, love, and renewed passion to push on because of these little reminders. Put them in your car, on your desk at work, in your wallet, so you never forget why you need to be strong and why you're called to overcome. They'll help you remember why you work hard to turn your pain into purpose and meaning. They'll find you when you're down and show you the kindness and compassion that you deserve. Regardless of what you may encounter, now you know that you can handle it and were made for it. Don't wish you had given everything to make your dreams come true, because there are people who depend on you.

IN LOVING MEMORY

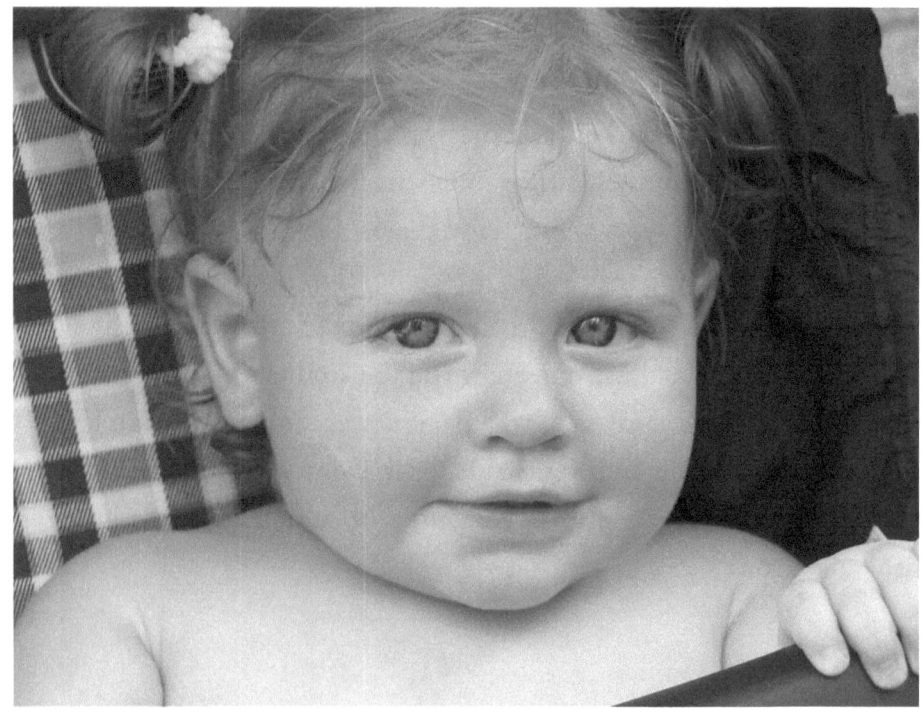

Madison Daley Funk (Maddie)
September 26, 2005 - October 23, 2007

Thank you so much for reading my book. Please check out some of these resources, which could be of great assistance to you.

www.maddiesmessage.com

https://www.parentsagainsttipovers.org/

Lifenethealth.org

https://www.consumerreports.org/home-garden/furniture-tip-over/sturdy-act-to-prevent-tip-overs-becomes-law-a5102433350/